Praise for *Cognitive Load The*

CW00504634

Teaching is one of the most important activities associated with the continuity o
of research relevant to teachers is produced each year, with the vast bulk of it ap͟   g ... ͟esearch journals
intended for a researcher rather than practitioner readership. Translating those technical research findings into a
form that is accessible to teachers is a rare skill. It is a skill that Steve Garnett has in copious abundance, and in
Cognitive Load Theory: A Handbook for Teachers he provides a brilliant exposition of instructional design principles. The
book has a consistent clarity of purpose and coherence that justifies a prominent place on every teacher's
bookshelf. I recommend it in the strongest possible terms.

John Sweller, Emeritus Professor of Educational Psychology, School of Education, University of New South Wales

Cognitive load theory is a hot topic in education at the moment – but, as with so much that gets introduced to
teachers, there is a risk of it being misunderstood and then mutating into something it was never meant to be.

Steve Garnett's book should ensure that cognitive load theory is fully understood by busy teachers. It brings a great
deal of clarity to a complex area of research and shows how it can be applied in the classroom to help teachers
make informed decisions about the way they design their lessons.

Mark Enser, Head of Geography and Research Lead, Heathfield Community College,
and author of *Teach Like Nobody's Watching* and *Powerful Geography*

I think it's safe to say that Steve Garnett's *Cognitive Load Theory: A Handbook for Teachers* is the book that educators have been waiting for. It is a much-needed, timely resource that puts common sense and cognitive science, rather than hunches and fashions, at the heart of the profession.

There are numerous books which now exist which demonstrate how teachers can take back control and strip away the ineffective nonsense, which of course make liberal reference to cognitive load theory. However, this book, dedicated entirely to the idea that working memory is limited, seeks to delve deeper into this theory. Garnett breaks cognitive load theory down into 14 different effects which impact on a range of stages of students' learning. Each of these are explained using clear, illustrated examples. Crucially, guidance is given that allows the teacher to consider how to adjust his or her lessons in light of these effects in order to maximise students' understanding and learning.

With input from cognitive load theory's main proponent, John Sweller, this book is a must-read for any educator seeking to improve their practice in line with the most up-to-date research.

Sarah Larsen, geography teacher, blogger and speaker

Cognitive Load Theory

A handbook for teachers

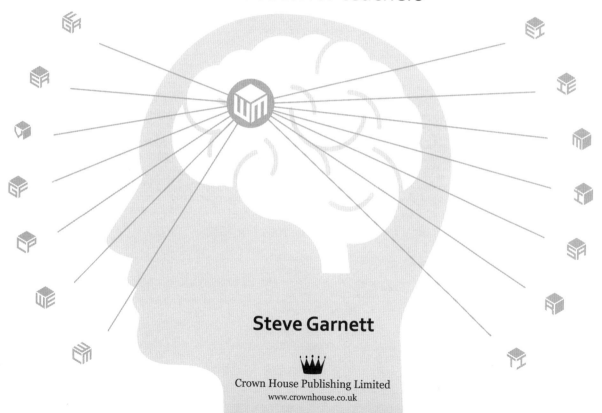

Steve Garnett

Crown House Publishing Limited
www.crownhouse.co.uk

First published by

Crown House Publishing Limited, Crown Buildings, Bancyfelin, Carmarthen, Wales, SA33 5ND, UK
www.crownhouse.co.uk

and

Crown House Publishing Company LLC, PO Box 2223, Williston, VT 05495, USA
www.crownhousepublishing.com

© Steve Garnett, 2020.

The right of Steve Garnett to be identified as the author of this work has been asserted by him in accordance with the Copyright, Designs and Patents Act 1988.

First published 2020.

Cover, geometric alphabet © Rodin Anton – stock.adobe.com; cover and page 4, head image © Fayee – stock.adobe.com;
page 5, brain image © mayboro95 – stock.adobe.com; pages 71, 79 and 80, violin image © Jan – stock.adobe.com;
pages 76–77, heart image © MariLee – stock.adobe.com; pages 81 and 83, palm-tree images © juliars – stock.adobe.com.

Crown House Publishing has no responsibility for the persistence or accuracy of URLs for external or third-party websites referred to in this publication, and does not guarantee that any content on such websites is, or will remain, accurate or appropriate.

British Library Cataloguing-in-Publication Data

A catalogue entry for this book is available from the British Library.

Print ISBN 978-178583501-8
Mobi ISBN 978-178583519-3
ePub ISBN 978-178583520-9
ePDF ISBN 978-178583521-6

LCCN 2020943344

Printed and bound in the UK by
Charlesworth Press, Wakefield, West Yorkshire

Acknowledgements

There is no doubt that I am hugely indebted to Emeritus Professor John Sweller for his guidance during the writing of this book. He is, ultimately, the principle reason why this book was written.

I remember clearly the moment when I decided to take the somewhat impulsive decision to find his academic email address via a Google search, which ultimately took me to the University of New South Wales in Australia. From there I wrote a hopeful email wondering if he had the time to have a look at what I had written with a view to possibly offering some pointers as to how it might be improved.

He kindly responded to my email (much to my amazement!) and wrote some very kind words too. From there he continued to review the book as it progressed. As he is the world's leading authority on this topic, naturally, I waited with bated breath for his emails to arrive. It's to his credit that they were both hugely encouraging and motivational as well as precise and focused as to how the book could be even better.

He had a huge influence on the final version of the book. Thank you, John.

I would also like to thank the team at Crown House Publishing. My thanks go to managing director David Bowman for saying 'yes'! I would also like to thank Louise Penny for her constructive comments at the editing stage of the process. There is no doubt that the book improved immeasurably through her insights, observations and, of course, corrections!

Having written an award-nominated book for Crown House Publishing before, I know that the marketing efforts of Rosalie Williams will be such that as many teachers as possible will get to hear about cognitive load theory. Thanks.

Preface

I have a picture in my mind of the intended readership of this book. It's the busy teacher, possibly teaching an overcrowded curriculum in an overcrowded classroom.

This book is for the teacher who doesn't have the time – or, indeed, perhaps the inclination – to access the original journals or research papers from which this book ultimately draws. Therefore, there is a deliberate approach to style and substance taken in this book, which is to make the theory accessible, practical and ready to be implemented almost immediately.

In short, it's meant to save time for teachers everywhere.

Contents

Acknowledgements i

Preface iii

Introduction 1

Where did CLT originate? 2

What does this cognitive science mean
for teachers? 4

What types of cognitive load can be placed on
working memory? 12

How do I ensure that pupils experience the right
amount of cognitive load when learning
something new? 15

What are CLT effects and how do they relate to
cognitive load specifically? 16

In the classroom 23

Teaching point 1: Introducing a new topic **25**

Element interactivity effect 26

Isolated elements effect 28

Teaching a complex concept within an
individual lesson 34

Summary 68

**Teaching point 2: Teaching new
knowledge/skills** **69**

Modality effect 70

Imagination effect 74

Split-attention effect 75

Redundancy effect 81

Transient information effect 87

Summary 97

Teaching point 3: Checking for recall and understanding **93**

Collective working memory effect 94

Summary 99

Teaching point 4: Pupils demonstrate understanding **101**

Completion problem effect 105

Guidance-fading effect 106

Variability effect 107

Expertise reversal effect 110

Goal-free effect 111

Summary 115

Conclusion **117**

References and further reading 121

Introduction

I remember very clearly what I was thinking when I read a tweet that Professor Dylan Wiliam posted on 26 January 2017: a tweet that made a pretty emphatic claim.

> **I've come to the conclusion Sweller's Cognitive Load Theory is the single most important thing that teachers should know.**[1]

My thinking was quite simple: 'I have absolutely no idea what that is!'

I spend my professional life working with teachers to improve all aspects of the learning experience for their pupils. Over the last 12–15 years my work has extended to over 30 countries around the world, including extensive experience across the whole of the UK. When I count the number of workshops and whole-school or whole-staff professional development sessions I have run, the number of teachers I have delivered training to must extend to over 15,000 quite easily.

My point in telling you this is that, up until I saw the Dylan Wiliam tweet, the concept of cognitive load theory (CLT) had never, ever come up. It was never a question raised when training teachers, never came up within a wider, more general conversation related to aspects of pedagogy, nor was it ever requested as a focus for training.

In short, my view was that whilst I certainly had no idea about CLT, teachers – whether working in the primary or secondary sector, whether in state or independent schools, or international schools across the world – had no idea either.

So when a claim as emphatic as Wiliam's is made about something, I feel I should not only find out what

---

1   D. Wiliam, Twitter, 26 January 2017. Available at: https://twitter.com/dylanwiliam/status/824682504602943489.

it is all about (for my own sake!), but, more importantly, I need to put any new knowledge I gain together so that busy teachers can use these insights to improve their pupils' learning experiences.

What follows is an attempt to bridge the research base of this theory and show how to put it into practice by describing and demonstrating what should be happening in real classrooms with real pupils when the principles of CLT are embedded.

You might – as I did – have some preliminary questions about CLT, so we'll begin by exploring those.

Where did CLT originate?

Emeritus Professor John Sweller, of the University of New South Wales, Australia, conceived of the theory of CLT and published a paper on it in April 1988.[2] Sweller himself says that after this his work was largely ignored for the next 20 years! Dylan Wiliam's tweet suggests that the theory had remained largely confined to narrow academic fields, and was certainly not at home in the pedagogical discourse with which normal classroom teachers were familiar.

Sweller's theory was used to generate hypotheses that were investigated by teams of researchers around the world and tested using randomised controlled trials. The efficacy of CLT rests on a base of hundreds of these randomised controlled trials, testing many thousands of primary and secondary schoolchildren as well as adults.

CLT can be described as something of a 'moving target' in the sense that Sweller has been constantly evolving and updating the theory since that first publication in the late 1980s, as we'll see on the timeline of major developments on pages 18–19. It has also been influenced by new thinking and studies by other researchers. One such example of external influence was as a result of David Geary's work on

---

2   J. Sweller, Cognitive Load During Problem Solving: Effects on Learning, *Cognitive Science: A Multidisciplinary Journal*, 12(2) (1988): 257–285.

evolutionary educational psychology.[3] Briefly, Geary made a distinction in terms of how the brain processes and organises information, dividing it into two spheres:

1. That which can only be learnt.

The first aspect Geary terms 'biologically primary knowledge'. This relates to all the things the brain does which cannot be formally taught. Essentially things like how to communicate in our first language and how to recognise faces. These things, he says, are just learnt and cannot be formally taught. It's an evolutionary thing.

2. That which can only be taught.

The second is termed 'biologically secondary knowledge'. This is all the things we need to learn in order to function successfully as human beings in society. Examples can include everything from learning how to count or read, to learning how to ride a bike or change a plug.

This is where schools come in. They are tasked with the purpose of passing on 'biologically secondary' skills to pupils. Sweller describes the differences beautifully when he says that (broadly) reading and writing can only be taught, whilst speaking and listening can only be learnt.

Sweller adds a slight adjustment in recognising that, across the curriculum, what needs to be learnt in maths is clearly different to what needs to be learnt in English, so he introduces the phrase 'domain-specific biologically secondary knowledge'.[4] This type of knowledge needs to be taught formally and explicitly to pupils – expressed through the phrase 'explicit instruction'.

In this model, the pupil is the 'novice' and the teacher is the 'expert', so passing knowledge from the expert to the novice can be seen as the role of the teacher.

---

3   D. C. Geary, *Origin of Mind: Evolution of Brain, Cognition, and General Intelligence* (Washington, DC: American Psychological Association, 2005).

4   J. Sweller, Cognitive Load Theory, without an Understanding of Human Cognitive Architecture, Instruction is Blind, talk given at researchED Melbourne (3 July 2017). Available at: https://www.youtube.com/watch?v=gOLPfi9Ls-w.

Geary's model made total sense to Sweller. It revealed the reason for the struggles that we have when trying to learn biologically secondary knowledge. It's because we are not (in evolutionary terms) designed to learn this knowledge naturally: so we must be taught it.

What does this cognitive science mean for teachers?

Sweller's big idea is that the brain has a very specific way of processing the learning of *new* or *novel* domain-specific biologically secondary knowledge. Once a teacher understands how this system works, they can improve the quality of instruction that a pupil receives. If the teacher doesn't understand the system that the brain uses to process this type of new learning, then the quality of learning is hampered.

This is why Sweller describes CLT as an 'instructional theory': by understanding it, teachers will be better able to deliver quality instruction.

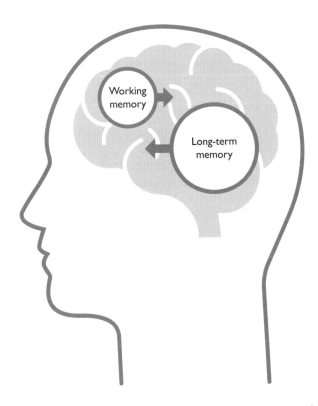

Figure I.1: The two major components of Sweller's information processing system

The information processing system Sweller describes has two major components, as shown in Figure I.1. Figure I.2 then reveals a little more about how working memory and long-term memory function.

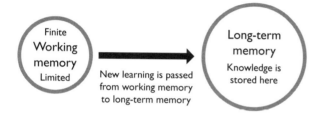

Figure I.2: Sweller's information processing system for new, domain-specific biologically secondary knowledge

Working memory

Figure I.3 (see page 6) locates the position of working memory, towards the front of the brain. In neurological terms it's in the central executive part of the prefrontal cortex. It's smaller in size than the part of the brain that stores long-term memories (further

back in the brain the hippocampus acts as the trigger for long-term memories).

Working memory is the part of the brain that processes what we are currently doing and thinking. If that is completely new or novel, then we can only deal with a *finite* amount of information at one time.

How much is a finite amount? Let's take this example: you make a mental list of 20 items that you need to buy at the supermarket. Sweller agrees with what cognitive psychologist George A. Miller coined as the 'Magical Number Seven'. Miller's paper of that name was published in 1956, but the figure still seems to hold true.[5] In other words, most people would only recall around seven items from the shopping list. Some might recall as few as five but others as many as nine – hence the full title of this oft-cited paper: 'The Magical Number Seven, Plus or Minus Two'.

5   G. A. Miller, The Magical Number Seven, Plus or Minus Two: Some Limits on Our Capacity for Processing Information, *Psychological Review*, 63(2) (1956): 81–97.

The other 13 items in the shopping list you would likely have forgotten about around 20 seconds after thinking about them. In other words, that memory is *limited* in duration.

However, Sweller goes on to say that if what you are trying to hold in your working memory has what he calls 'element interactivity' – or, in other words, the pieces of novel information are interconnected or linked in some way that is a bit more complicated and involved – then working memory has even less capacity to remember, so the number would drop to three or four items.

Essentially, working memory acts as a 'gatekeeper' to new learning.

The implications for the classroom teacher are clear. When teaching a class of pupils a new topic or skill, the teacher must be aware of both the limitations of the working memory and how it functions, because it is this part of the brain that will be attending to all the new learning.

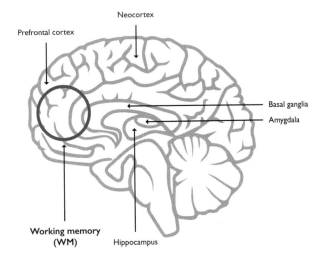

Figure 1.3: Location of working memory within the brain

Sweller is really clear on the implications of the limitations on working memory:

> **The implications of working memory limitations on instructional design can hardly be overestimated. [...] Anything beyond the simplest cognitive activities appear to overwhelm working memory. Prima facie, any instructional design that flouts or merely ignores working memory limitations inevitably is deficient.**[6]

Long-term memory

In contrast, the long-term memory is described by Sweller as 'indescribably large' and something that 'nobody's measured'.[7] He argues that the main objective behind teachers understanding and using CLT in their practice is for pupils to have, ultimately, a greater store of knowledge in their long-term memory. In order to form a memory, the brain must store any new information so that it can be accessed again later, which it does through a process called 'encoding'. There are broadly three ways in which new learning transitions from working memory to long-term memory: acoustic, visual and semantic.

Here is a simple example.

Acoustic encoding: Imagine that you are introduced to someone for the first time and you don't know their name. Their first name is Jane. Once they are introduced as Jane that information would transition

6   J. Sweller, J. J. G. van Merrienboer and F. G. W. C. Paas, Cognitive Architecture and Instructional Design, *Educational Psychology Review*, 10(3) (1998): 251–296 at 252–253.

7   J. Sweller, Cognitive Load Theory, without an Understanding of Human Cognitive Architecture, Instruction is Blind.

from working memory to long-term memory through the process of hearing it said.

The way to ensure that you would then keep that person's first name in your long-term memory would be through rehearsal. Repeat the name frequently to make it 'stick'.

Visual encoding: Cognitive scientists would explain this as the process of converting things that you see into mental images. Similarly, when you see something new or novel, it means that you are likely to remember it. The maxim 'I never forget a face' probably holds true as it would be an example of visual encoding (Perhaps this is quite obvious, but nonetheless it is how encoding works.)

Semantic encoding: Again, cognitive scientists suggest that if new sensory information can be linked to existing knowledge or understanding then it is better remembered. When you make sense of something and see how it functions or operates then this allows semantic encoding to take place. So the word 'polygon' with no context will be difficult for a novice learner to remember but if an association is

made to it, in this case a drawing of a polygon, then the chances of it being remembered are higher.

The goal of learning should not be to acquire a whole lot of unrelated facts or items of knowledge, but rather a collection of these facts and items of knowledge. They then should be interconnected and relatable to each other in order to build greater coherence and depth of understanding.

Encoding places this new learning in long-term memory. As pupils acquire new learning and then relate it to existing knowledge, then it can be said that the process of schema acquisition has begun.

The ultimate ambition is to develop well-constructed, coherent and detailed schema within our pupils' minds. Well-thought-out teaching ultimately guides pupils to building schemas.

Schemas

A schema organises elements of information according to how they will be used and can be relatively simple or complex.

Examples of possible schemas include:

Alphabet.

Number line.

Mathematical/scientific formula.

Dictionary.

Encyclopaedia.

Chapters in a book.

Instructions on how to build a bookcase.

Dance routine.

Mark scheme.

Bus timetable.

Musical notation.

A tactical plan.

Knowing how to drive a car.

Solving number problems.

Labelled diagram.

Graphic organiser.

Knowledge and understanding are interconnected because knowledge is the collection of different concepts, ideas and facts, whilst understanding is the connections made between them.

Schemas are crucial to pupils' understanding because of the importance of these connections.

The goal of the teacher is, firstly, to help pupils to construct schemas, both by initially instructing pupils (presenting the knowledge) and then by building up the complexity of the schema (securing the pupils' understanding). This way pupils are not just remembering a series of unrelated statements, facts or skills. Given that a schema can take a variety of forms such as a number line or alphabet or formula or essay plan, the role of the teacher in part is to teach the schema (e.g. numbers 1–10) in the correct order. The next job of the teacher is to assist pupils in getting these schemas automated (recalled without hesitation) so that they can be readily, easily and quickly retrieved and applied.

There are definitely some schools of thought which assume that transferring knowledge into long-term memory requires nothing other than 'rote learning' or 'drilling' – potentially a pejorative term, meaning that nothing is understood, just recalled. In other words, we end up with the unthinking pupil who can remember something but not understand it.

An example of this might be a pupil who can recall that the chemical symbol for iron is Fe. In fact, they can do this for most of the elements in the periodic table.

Sweller completely sees the value of storing knowledge – in fact, as much knowledge as possible – in the long-term memory. Providing, of course, that the knowledge is attached to a useful schema.

So, in this example, Sweller would prefer to see not only the ability to recall the correct chemical symbol for iron and the rest of the elements, but also that the

pupil knows where each element is located in the periodic table, and why, based on its mass or whether or not it's a metal. Understanding the periodic table in this way is an example of having a schema.

Pupils' ability to automate detailed recall of such schemas is, Sweller argues, the real 'prize'. Indeed, he describes it as transformational. The key point is this:

> **Ultimately the route to genuine competency in anything that needs to be learnt is via secure recall of the appropriate schema, located in long-term memory.**

Sweller points to research done on chess grandmasters, comparing their game play with that of a 'weekend player'. He asks what separates the two groups in terms of their competence as chess players.

The obvious conclusion might be that the grandmaster has an incredible intellect which is used to work out the best moves and strategy to beat their opponent.

The real answer turns out to be something of the opposite!

Grandmasters' success is simply down to the fact that they have a powerful memory of the different configurations possible on a chess board (this is, essentially, their schema). Once they recognise the configuration in front of them, they know the best moves to make in order to win. In short, it is their recall of configurations that singles them out and nothing else.

So this would be why Daniel T. Willingham, professor of psychology at the University of Virginia, said 'understanding is remembering in disguise'.[8]

This is a brilliant quote that should hopefully persuade those who might believe that knowledge recall is just a low-end cognitive challenge.

Analogies can often be useful devices to help communicate concepts. What follows is one that

sprung to my mind to help get across the structure of the brain's information processing system as described by Sweller. It is based on a bookshelf and a library.

Imagine putting up a new – very small – bookshelf in the entrance hallway of a house, by the front door (this mirrors the idea that working memory lies at the front of the brain and is where the brain first processes 'new' knowledge). This bookshelf can only hold three to five books (depending on their thickness). Trying to put more books on the shelf will mean that some of them will fall off because the bookshelf is too small to hold anymore (mirroring the problem of limited working memory capacity).

8   D. T. Willingham, *Why Don't Students Like School? A Cognitive Scientist Answers Questions About How the Mind Works and What It Means for the Classroom* (San Francisco, CA: Jossey-Bass, 2009), p. 88.

Let's now develop the analogy further so that it links to the notion of knowledge transfer from working memory to long-term memory.

Imagine that you have decided to build a library in one of the rooms at the back of the house. Once the books on the hallway shelf have been read, they can then be put in the library for the long term, ready to be accessed at any point in the future. The library in this analogy, of course, being long-term memory. (This movement of the books from the shelf at the front of the house to the library at the back of the house, for long-term storage and to be accessible at any future point, mirrors the idea of the transfer-ence of new knowledge from working memory to long-term memory.)

Sweller argues that being competent or lacking competence in something depends entirely on how secure the retrieval of knowledge held in the schema is.

What types of cognitive load can be placed on working memory?

It is now generally accepted that there are two types of cognitive load: intrinsic and extrinsic. Sweller effectively disregarded what had previously been considered a third type – germane load – in 2010, so as a result no further reference will be made to it in this book. As he says:

Unlike intrinsic and extraneous cognitive load, germane cognitive load does not constitute an independent source of cognitive load. It merely refers to the

working memory resources available to deal with the element interactivity associated with intrinsic cognitive load.[9]

Intrinsic load

Intrinsic cognitive load relates to the inherent difficulty of the material itself. Sweller developed this concept when trying to understand why some of his experiments worked and some didn't, even though they were testing the same thing. It was the result of a variance in the complexity of what was being processed.

So if the new content to be learnt is inherently detailed and complex, with lots of 'moving parts', then it stands to reason that pupils can quickly be overwhelmed by this, thus exceeding their working memory capacity. Sweller is clear that if something is new but easy to remember (such as the sum $2 + 2 = 4$) then there will be low intrinsic load. However, learning something like a quadratic equation – which has more elements to it that need to be held in working memory simultaneously – will result in a higher intrinsic load.

In other words, more complex content with lots of element interactivity will place a high cognitive load on pupils. This type of load is sometimes described as 'good' load, because the teacher would not want to make content too easy at the expense of exposing pupils to higher value, more complex content. Ultimately, we want our pupils to be able to learn that which is complex and detailed. The challenge is to make it challenging enough but not so challenging that it becomes too much.

Therefore we are aiming for *high load* but still within working memory limits so as not to cause overload.

---

9   J. Sweller, Element Interactivity and Intrinsic, Extraneous, and Germane Cognitive Load, *Educational Psychology Review*, 22(2), Cognitive Load Theory: New Conceptualizations, Specifications, and Integrated Research Perspectives (2010): 123–138 at 126.

Extraneous load

Extraneous cognitive load is the load generated *by the way in which* the material is presented and relates to anything which does not aid learning. Originally Sweller saw all overload as extraneous load. Learning materials can be unintentionally delivered and presented in such a way that it actually exceeds pupils' working memory capacity because there is too much badly designed information and it is hard for pupils to deal with and filter out the relevant parts.

For teachers, 90% of the story behind reducing cognitive load on working memory revolves around addressing issues related to extraneous load.

We need low extraneous load so that space can be freed up for higher intrinsic load (as shown in Figure I.4).

This analogy should help conceptualise the point. Imagine the perfect cup of takeaway cappuccino. It would contain a small amount of espresso coffee (extraneous load in this analogy) and the rest of the drink would be frothy milk (intrinsic load). Thus, this

describes the optimum mixture for the amount of load the novice learner can process (i.e. low extraneous load but the optimum intrinsic load – we don't want the cup to overflow, of course).

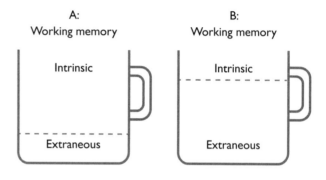

Figure I.4: Desirable and undesirable load

If our cup is already very full of strong coffee, we will have no room for the milk and our drink will be too bitter and hard to swallow for the untrained palate (novice learner). Desirable cognitive load is achieved by keeping any extraneous load to a minimum. This involves taking care with the instructional design of learning materials and the teacher exposition, thus keeping extraneous load as low as possible.

The right amount of challenge and complexity is achieved through careful attention to how difficult you make the acquisition of schemas, thus having a 'good' amount of intrinsic load.

This positive weighting in the balance between different types of load is summarised nicely by Paul A. Kirschner, professor of educational psychology at the Open University in the Netherlands, who suggested to:

> **Maximise useful load, minimise irrelevant load.**[10]

---

10 P. A. Kirschner, The Ideal Learning Environment: Evidence-Informed Strategies for EEE-Learning, presentation delivered at researchED National Conference (8 September 2018), quote on slide 15. Available at: https://researched.org.uk/wp-content/uploads/delightful-downloads/2018/09/Paul-Kirschner-rED18-The-Ideal-Learning-Environment.pdf.

How do I ensure that pupils experience the right amount of cognitive load when learning something new?

The teacher needs to essentially balance cognitive load in favour of the desirable at the expense of the undesirable.

This involves careful attention in terms of thinking about the complexity of your content and how you can make it accessible without oversimplifying it. Care will be needed regarding the design of worksheets and slides that deliver learning materials.

The teacher will also need to carefully consider how much support pupils receive. Knowing when to gradually remove any scaffolding will be important.

Lastly the teacher will need to reflect on the auditory dimension of the lesson. Specifically, the timing of teacher talk and the amount of it is crucial to understanding some aspects of undesirable load, expressed through different CLT effects.

They will then need to attempt to pitch the lesson content so that there is the right amount of intrinsic load.

What are CLT effects and how do they relate to cognitive load specifically?

Since the early 1980s, Sweller himself has directly researched, or overseen research into, a number of 'instructional techniques' or influences that affect instruction and, ultimately, cognitive load.

These have all been tested using randomised controlled trials and are expressed as 'effects'. This book focuses on 14 of them: some of which relate to intrinsic load and some to extraneous.

Figure 1.5 lists them in date order (see pages 18–19).

CLT effects linked to intrinsic load

The element interactivity effect is the one that led to the notion of intrinsic load. Teachers might be familiar with this term if they have searched online to find out more about CLT, as it is discussed in a lot of the literature. Intrinsic load relates to the inherent complexity of a subject or the content that a pupil needs to process. If element interactivity is too high, then working memory cannot process the necessary, most relevant information efficiently. The quest for the teacher is to get element interactivity just right. This is no easy feat!

CLT effects linked to extraneous load

Internet searches also reference extraneous load as a type of overload on working memory. The split-attention effect, redundancy effect, expertise reversal effect and transient information effect are all examples of effects that can 'clutter' working memory with unhelpful additional stimuli or 'noise', ultimately getting in the way of effective learning. Collectively these effects gave rise to the term 'extraneous load'.

Other effects, though, have been tested – and by understanding how best to utilise them in our teaching, we can avoid overloading working memory for our novice learners.

The 14 effects that Sweller and colleagues have studied are listed in the table on pages 20–21, with a brief description of each.

However, note that they are listed in the order in which we will encounter them in the remainder of the text.

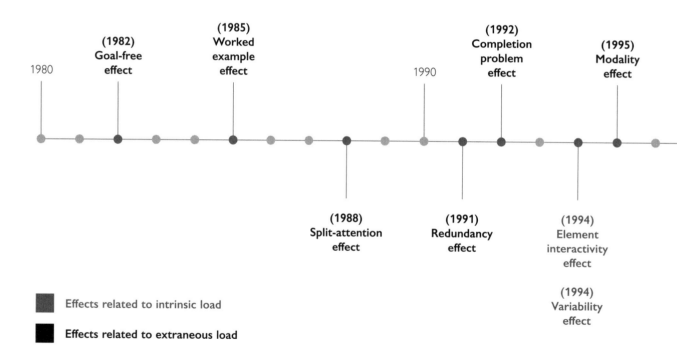

1980

(1982)
Goal-free
effect

(1985)
Worked
example
effect

1990

(1992)
Completion
problem
effect

(1995)
Modality
effect

(1988)
Split-attention
effect

(1991)
Redundancy
effect

(1994)
Element
interactivity
effect

(1994)
Variability
effect

Effects related to intrinsic load

Effects related to extraneous load

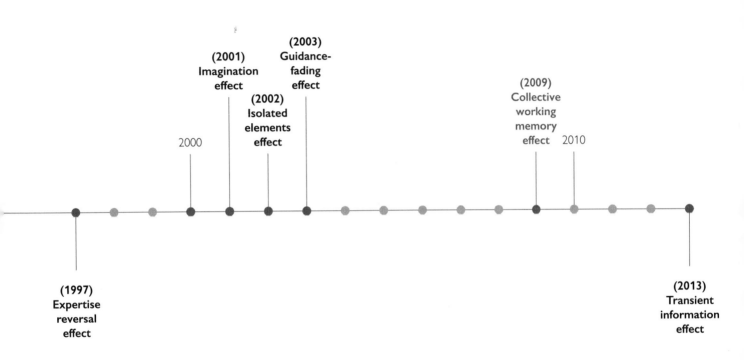

Figure 1.5: Chronology of the development of CLT

The 14 CLT effects

CLT effect	Abbreviation	Brief description
Element interactivity	EI	Describes the level of complexity involved in learning something new.
Isolated elements	IE	The process of separating out the individual components involved when learning something.
Modality	M	The combination of spoken words together with relevant images to support the teaching of something new.
Imagination	I	The visualisation of concepts or procedures into mental images to assist with better recall.
Split-attention	SA	Occurs when the relevant stimuli are spread out all over a page and force constant change in focus and eye movement.
Redundancy	R	Occurs when extraneous or repeated information is provided on the same page/slide/worksheet.
Transient information	TI	The negative impact on learning when too much verbal exposition comes from the teacher.

CLT effect	Abbreviation	Brief description
Collective working memory	CWM	The process of asking pupils to pool their working memories rather than just draw on their own more limited ones.
Worked example	WE	Providing an example or model of a successful piece of work in order for pupils to devote more mental resources to creating their own.
Completion problem	CP	Created by giving pupils an incomplete worked example and then asking them to work out the rest for themselves.
Guidance-fading	GF	The process of gradually reducing the level of scaffolding and support a pupil receives.
Variability	V	Showing pupils a range of worked examples before they begin their own work.
Expertise reversal	ER	Avoiding spoon-feeding pupils too much, especially as their expertise grows.
Goal-free	GFr	Minimising the amount of instructions pupils receive when processing information.

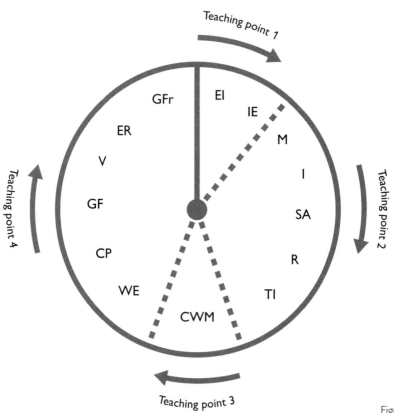

Figure I.6: Full teaching cycle

In the classroom

We will now consider when each of these 14 CLT effects might best be reflected upon when delivering a lesson or series of lessons.

Figure I.6 on page 22 promotes the idea that, when instructing the novice learner, it is helpful to break up the teaching process into a sequence of component parts.

Using the abbreviations from the table on pages 20–21, you can see when each of the 14 CLT effects might need to be considered within the four components of the lesson. Looking at the graphic, how easy do you find it to interpret this information? Can you recall what the abbreviations stand for? How many can you hold in your working memory? Do you need to look back at the list to make sense of this new information? Could I have presented this information differently? These are the kinds of questions we should be considering when designing learning materials and ways of presenting information.

The component parts of the lesson are described as 'teaching points', and there are four in total:

Teaching point 1: introducing a new topic.

Teaching point 2: teaching new knowledge/skills.

Teaching point 3: checking for recall and understanding.

Teaching point 4: pupils demonstrate understanding.

Broadly this involves an input phase (teaching points 1 and 2) in which formal instruction/teaching takes place. This is then followed by a crucial midway point at which the teacher can carry out some kind of informal assessment (teaching point 3) to gauge overall levels of understanding.

If the class has achieved a sufficiently high level of understanding (around 80%[11]), the teacher would then move into the final phase, in which pupils would be engaged in demonstrating their knowledge and

---

11 The notion of an optimal 80% success rate is taken from Barak Rosenshine's Principles of Instruction: Research-Based Strategies That Every Teacher Should Know, *American Educator* (Spring 2012): 12–19, 39 at 17. Available at: https://www.aft.org/sites/default/files/periodicals/Rosenshine.pdf.

understanding (teaching point 4). If levels of accurate understanding seem to be much lower than 80% – as indicated by the number of pupils answering questions incorrectly – then this would clearly signal to the teacher that there were significant omissions of knowledge and/or a lack of understanding. The teacher would therefore need to reteach the content delivered in teaching points 1 and 2.

Different CLT effects need to be considered at these various teaching points.

CLT is an instructional theory, so it follows that its structure supports a knowledge transmission model, at least in the early stages. The most effective learning for the novice occurs when the teacher acts as the expert and teaches the pupils directly.

There are, of course, other models – such as discovery learning or enquiry-based learning. Sweller is clear, though, that these models are most appropriate for pupils who are closer to the expert stage. Essentially, the expert does not experience the same working memory limitations as the novice does. The expert, therefore, has the necessary depth of knowledge stored in long-term memory to engage in independent learning.

CLT addresses the needs and perspective of the novice learner and so is an instructional model.

Teaching point 1

Introducing a new topic

CLT effects to consider:

Element interactivity effect (EI).

Isolated elements effect (IE).

When introducing a new topic it is important to be aware of both the element interactivity effect and the isolated elements effect.

The teacher needs to avoid asking pupils to process content that is too detailed and complex too early on in the new topic or lesson. If they offer complex information at the outset, the element interactivity may be too high.

Moreover, by breaking the content down into manageable chunks, and teaching it accordingly, the teacher is instead promoting the isolated elements effect, which will help to avoid overloading working memory.

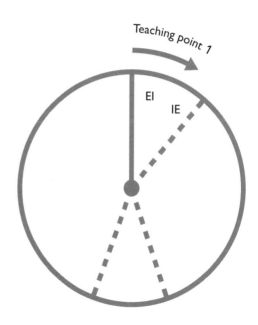

Figure 1.1: Teaching point 1

As a reminder, it is important to remember that the principles of CLT only apply to domain-specific biologically secondary knowledge. The 'rules' also only apply to the limitations in working memory which occur when the pupil is a novice, with very limited knowledge of a given topic. Their schema is, in effect, empty.

Element interactivity effect

Given this premise, let's take the example of a teacher who is preparing to teach the topic of polygons to a class of novice learners.

What would potentially be wrong with presenting the topic as shown in Figure 1.2 on page 27?

The answer to this question is that, in CLT terms, the problem is one of high element interactivity. Whilst it is still an example of a schema, there is too much detail in this resource for the novice learner to cope with, meaning working memory would be overwhelmed.

The focus of the learning is polygons. However, the relevant information is effectively hidden from the novice learner. It sits within a sea of content. The other information – angles, averages, fractions, decimals and percentages – will be relevant to pupils as they progress through the maths curriculum, but at the moment represents too much irrelevant detail for the novice.

There is also no apparent coherence within this resource – at least not for the novice learner. For example, pupils would have no sense of any common features, groupings or relationships between various polygons. The teacher (i.e. the expert) would clearly see this coherence, but the novice learner simply could not.

It is absolutely crucial to remember that the teacher would certainly want the pupils to know and understand all of this material at the *end* of the topic (and CLT recognises this). Pupils being able to recall and demonstrate precise and accurate understanding of the content in this schema is, of course, the ultimate goal. In the terminology of CLT, we'd call this the 'automation of schemas'.

Angles

full turn	360°
half turn	180°
right angle	90°
acute angle	<90°
obtuse angle	>90°
reflex angle	>180°
angles on a straight line	180°
angles inside a triangle	180°
angles inside a quadrilateral	360°

Polygons	No. of sides
quadrilateral	4
pentagon	5
hexagon	6
heptagon	7
octagon	8
nonagon	9
decagon	10

1/100	0.01	1%	÷ 100
1/20	0.05	5%	÷ 20
1/10	0.1	10%	÷ 10
1/5	0.2	20%	÷ 5
1/4	0.25	25%	÷ 4
1/2	0.5	50%	÷ 2
3/4	0.75	75%	÷ 4, ✗ 3
1	1	100%	÷ 1

The mean

The mean is a type of average. To find the mean, add up all the numbers and divide by how many there are. E.g. the mean of 4, 5, 3, 4 is 4 (This is because 4 + 5 + 3 + 4 = 16, and 16 ÷ 4 = 4)

Fractions, decimals and percentages

Term	Definition	Example
factor	a number that divides exactly into another number	factors of 12 = 1, 2, 3, 4, 6, 12
common factor	factors that are shared by two or more numbers	common factors of 8 and 12 = 1, 2, 4
prime number	a number with only 2 factors: 1 and itself	2, 3, 5, 7, 11, 13, 17, 19 …
composite number	a number with more than two factors	12 (it has 6 factors)
prime factor	a factor that is prime	prime factors of 12 = 2, 3
multiple	a number in another's times table	multiples of 9 = 9, 18, 27, 36
common multiples	multiples that are shared by two or more numbers	common multiples of 4 and 6 = 12, 24
square number	the result when a number has been multiplied by itself	25 (5 x 5) 49 (7 x 7)
cube number	the result when a number has been multiplied by itself three times	8 (2 x 2 x 2) 27 (3 x 3 x 3)

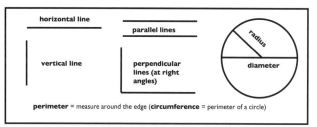

horizontal line

parallel lines

vertical line

perpendicular lines (at right angles)

radius

diameter

perimeter = measure around the edge (**circumference** = perimeter of a circle)

Figure 1.2: Option A – expert

One of the issues with schemas like this example is that they are written by the expert but not seen through the eyes of the novice.

Therefore, in CLT terms, it would be highly erroneous to *start* with this.

Isolated elements effect

Let's now approach this topic in a CLT-friendly way.

For the novice learner, it would be more effective if the content on polygons was instead designed in the way shown in Figure 1.3 on page 29.

The question is, why?

This second option promotes the isolated elements effect, and is therefore desirable. Essentially, the teacher would deal with each element in turn. Through direct instruction the pupils would learn everything they need to know about the properties of these polygons.

The experienced teacher who is introducing the topic of polygons would probably start with the four-sided shapes. Of these, the square would be the first, as it contains the least number of variables (i.e. the sides are the same length, all the angles are the same and there is minimal variation of numbers – e.g. the length is the same as the width).

The teacher would offer direct instruction about the properties of the square first and promote understanding, perhaps through worked examples. They would not only ensure that pupils have understood but would also try to obtain a high success rate – indicated, for example, by correct answers to informal assessment questions. Only then would the teacher progress onto the next shape, such as the rhombus.

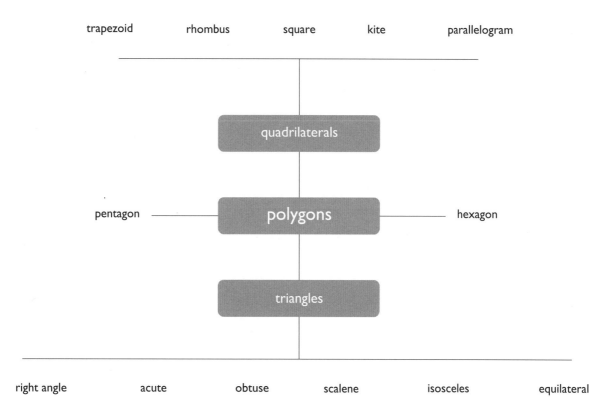

Figure 1.3: Option B – novice

The teacher may attempt to reduce cognitive load even further. Here they could hide all the other words from the class, except the one which they are focusing on – in this case 'square'. The teacher asks the class to focus on only one word, and thereby avoids any distractions which might be generated by having the other words on the knowledge schema revealed to them.

As the teacher progresses through the topic, then the other polygon shapes on the schema would be revealed.

There are three key characteristics present in the novice schema that should be taken into account if a teacher is thinking about designing their own such schema to use with novice learners.

1. Ensure that it is full of appropriate tier 3 vocabulary. These are those domain-specific technical terms that are only really used in reference to this topic. (So for polygons, examples would be trapezoid or parallelogram – and, indeed, polygon.) Pupils are less likely to have come across tier 3 words in any other context (i.e. their schema

is empty), so these need to be explained clearly. Tier 2 words, on the other hand, are academic words which are used regularly across subject domains, whilst tier 1 words are everyday words which are common to the majority of pupils.[1] Tier 2 or tier 1 words would only be included in the schema if they are fundamental to that topic – for example, the word 'square'.

2. Communicate any hierarchies, groups or themes clearly and visually. Use linking lines and shaded boxes to do this. (For example, it is clear that 'quadrilaterals' is the heading for the subgroup of words above it. They are linked and connected by lines to show this relationship.)

3. Think 'less can be more' and resist the temptation to overfill the schema, as happened in the expert version (Figure 1.2).

---

1   For a full discussion of vocabulary tiers see: I. L. Beck, M. G. McKeown and L. Kucan, *Bringing Words to Life: Robust Vocabulary Instruction*, 2nd edn (New York: The Guilford Press, 2013).

Once pupils have gained some fluency in understanding this topic then they can eventually be exposed to the expert schema. This is because the pupils are moving towards the expert end of the novice–expert continuum.

These two cognitive load effects perhaps suggest the need for the teacher to critique the resources that they present to their pupils during the course of their everyday teaching.

In this second example, a business studies teacher is going to focus on the topic of globalisation.

The first resource (Figure 1.4, on page 32) would be guilty of allowing element interactivity to be too high.

Instead, the teacher should choose to focus on the isolated elements effect and amend the resource to only show the part which is relevant to their class at that point. They should also use connecting lines carefully.

In the novice example (Figure 1.5 on page 33), we can see how the presentation conveys the idea that there are five pros of locating a business abroad and five cons.

This structure makes it easier for the teacher to adopt a 'small steps' approach with the class.

UNIT 2: BUSINESS INFLUENCES Ethical and environmental considerations

Ethics involves treating workers, suppliers and customers right; however, what is right and wrong evolves over time, so it can be hard for businesses to keep up.

Ethical marketing
Marketing activities that seek to give customers information to make good choices.

Environmentally friendly
Describes consumers and businesses that act to make production sustainable.

Sustainable production
Production that can be environmentally kept going.

Globalisation
The process by which business activity around the world has become increasingly interconnected.

Benefits of being environmentally friendly

Increased sales	Reduced costs
Reduced tax bills	Reduced resource scarcity

Economic climate
Refers to how well the country is doing in terms of the levels of income and employment.

Pros of a UK business locating abroad	**Cons of a UK business locating abroad**
Lower labour costs	Quality control
Lower costs	Poor communications
Expertise	Transport
Skilled workers	Loss of UK sales
Demand	Costs of moving

Influences on business

Ethical and environmental considerations
There could be negative implications if businesses don't follow UK guidelines in other countries.
The economic climate
This will influence whether or not a business is willing to operate there – if low income, the business will suffer.

International branding
Creating an image or values for a product in different countries.
Multinational companies
Businesses that operate in different countries.
Productivity
A measure of output of each worker on average.

Income
The amount of money people receive from work.
Customers
Buyers of goods and services.
Consumer income
The total amount a consumer earns through investments or work.
Gross domestic product (GDP)
A monetary measure of the goods and products a country produces.

Figure 1.4: Globalisation schema – expert

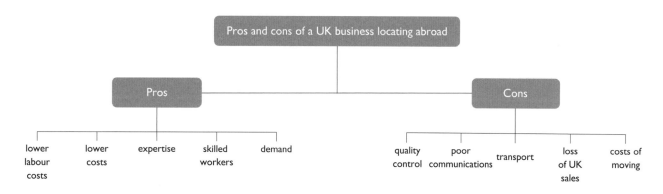

Figure 1.5: Globalisation schema – novice

Teaching a complex concept within an individual lesson

Naturally, it is also important to consider the implications of high element interactivity within the lesson as a whole.

Even though the teacher may have adopted a chunking approach to delivering the topic to ease cognitive load, there will still be occasions when a particularly tricky concept will surface that could, in itself, be too difficult for the novice pupils to grasp.

It's at moments like this when it's important to remember the benefits of the isolated elements effect.

Returning to maths, let's use the example of a pupil being tasked with calculating the area of a rectangle. For the novice, there would be several things to think about at once — for example, lengths, the formula and calculations. Potentially, it could be too much of a burden on working memory (i.e. there is too much element interactivity).

The solution would be to take an isolated elements approach.

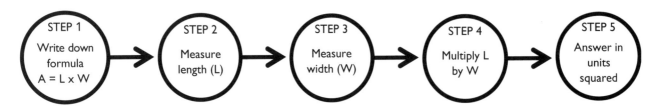

Figure 1.6: Pattern B — area calculation

A flow chart could be a useful teaching tool here, and this is another example of a type of schema (see Figure 1.6 on page 34). The teacher would go through each step involved in the calculation, such as measuring the length of one side of the rectangle in turn, aiming for a high success rate in terms of pupils being able to successfully complete each step.

Our previous example on polygons is perfect for this topic. However, how would the teacher proceed if the lesson has a different, and more complex, topic focus?

Such examples might be:

Teaching about the four stages of the lifecycle of a butterfly.

The causes and effects of deforestation in the Amazon rainforest.

The similarities and differences between animal cells and plant cells.

The answer would be to configure the shapes and lines in such a way as to visually represent the relationship between the elements that the pupils need to understand.

Diagrams which do this are called graphic organisers and are another form of schema. A graphic organiser is simply any configuration of lines and shapes that, when combined, attempt to create a visual representation of a pattern of thinking.

Graphic organisers are a helpful tool to use to overcome working memory limitations; they offer key aids to interpretation of meaning and understanding.

The patterns of thinking that will be considered here are:

A. Knowledge/recall.

B. Sequencing.

C. Cause and effect.

D. Similarities and differences.

E. Classification.

F. Connection.

Before showing some illustrative subject-specific examples, the following activity should serve as evidence of the efficacy of these graphic organisers as not only a tool for learning but also, specifically, as a means of avoiding overload in working memory.

This might best be done with a group of colleagues. You will ask them to read a passage of text to themselves. Warn them in advance that they will be given three questions to answer about the text.

The key to conducting the experiment effectively is this.

Ask them to read the text first without letting them see the questions you are going to be asking them. Then remove the text from sight and read out question 1.

Give them about 3–4 seconds to answer and ask them to write the answer on a piece of paper. The key is that you don't want them to read the text in order to answer the question but, of course, to use their memory instead.

Now reveal the text once again, informing them that they will be given a second question. Remove the text from view so that they have to rely on their working

memory. Proceed to read out question 2. Again, give them 3–4 seconds to think of an answer and ask them to write it down.

Now instruct them to read the text once again. Then read out question 3 and give them 3–4 seconds to think of an answer and write it down. Don't forget to remove the text from sight before you ask the question!

This is the text:

Ahmed is head of school. Moona is head of maths. Umair, Abdul and Rafa work for Moona. Khalid is the head of physics. Bazir, Rania and Rabah report to Khalid. Umair, Bazir, Rania and Khalid are working together on the joint preparing-for-university project.

These are the three questions:

1. Who is the highest-ranking individual on the preparing-for-university project?

2. Which department has the most staff members working on the preparing-for-university project?

3. Which staff members are not involved in the preparing-for-university project?

These are the answers to the three questions:

1. Khalid.

2. Physics.

3. Ahmed, Moona, Rafa, Abdul and Rabah.

What should happen is that they find it very difficult indeed to simultaneously hold in their minds all the necessary details from the text, whilst processing the question that has been asked and also searching mentally for the answer. Consequently (and hopefully) most will get all or most of the answers wrong!

The reason why they should get the answers wrong is that you are deliberately trying to overwhelm working memory!

Reinforce the idea that because they are, in effect, novices (i.e. they will not have any prior knowledge about the details in the text), this exercise should have overloaded their working memory. It might be a timely reminder too that their pupils will face this type of frustration and confusion whenever they are learning something new.

The optimum solution to avoid overwhelming working memory, enabling the participants to answer these three questions correctly, is simple.

Present the information contained in the text in a visual format, as shown in Figure 1.7 (page 38):

The same three questions are now so much easier to answer because you have combined the use of colour coding (the grey shaded box connects everyone working on the preparing-for-university project) with a representation of the hierarchy in the school.

Look back at the questions again, but this time use the visual to answer them and it should be a lot easier!

There are other reasons why graphic organisers work so well, and they lie with Gestalt theory.

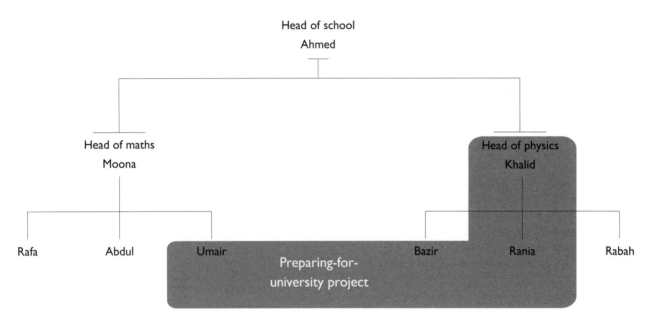

Figure 1.7: Preparing-for-university project

Briefly, in the early 20th century, three German psychologists – Max Wertheimer, Wolfgang Köhler, and Kurt Koffka – began studying visual perception within the brain. They concluded that the brain sees things as a whole, rather than as individual parts. The brain seeks to find patterns and forge links and associations, often by the positioning and configuration of lines and shapes. There are certain fundamentals that Gestalt theory proposes that we should think about when designing graphic organisers. These are:

Simplicity.

Symmetry.

Proximity.

Similarity.

Continuity.

Simplicity is achieved through avoiding the over-elaborate use of images and too much detail.

Symmetry is achieved through arranging groups in a systematic way with ordered alignments.

Proximity is achieved by ensuring that anything which is interrelated is kept close together.

Similarity is achieved through keeping things that are related together under relevant themes or headings and separate from that which is themed differently.

Continuity is achieved with the use of connecting lines. These lines can vary in thickness as they correspond to the relative importance of a connection, and the lines do not have to connect all the way. As long as it's clear where the final destination of the line is, sometimes the brain will connect an incomplete line to its final destination.

The following example attempts to illustrate Gestalt theory.

How do you think your brain interprets this diagram?

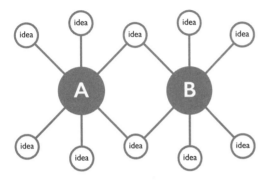

Figure 1.8: A and B shared values

Gestalt theorists would say that the rules of continuity and similarity are primarily present here. As a result, the brain would detect a pattern and relationship whereby four ideas are connected to value A only and four ideas are connected to value B only. There are also two ideas connected to both value A and value B (due to connecting lines). Therefore, the reading of this diagram instantly reveals that values A and B have both similarities (two of them) and differences (four each).

It might seem obvious to us as to what this diagram is communicating, but Gestalt theory explains why it is so.

We can see how graphic organisers can be highly effective tools to overcome working memory limitations. They can communicate almost instantly what might otherwise have to be communicated in lengthier written prose.

It is possible to communicate the same information but using far fewer working memory resources.

In the example shown in Figure 1.9 on page 41, the principle explained here is applied to a real teaching situation. In this case a biology teacher wants their pupils to identify similarities and differences between human and plant cells when studying organelles. They haven't studied this topic yet, so they are novices.

CLT would promote the use of this type of graphic organiser as the schema of choice. The teacher would constantly reference this resource as they guide their class through the ways in which plant and human cells are similar but also different.

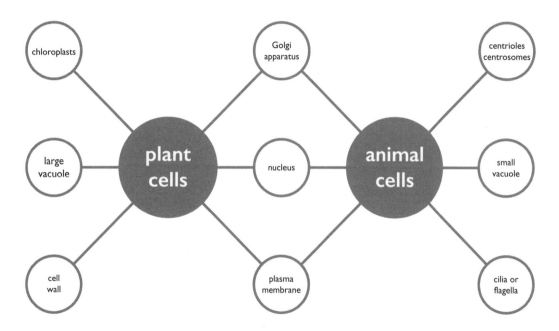

Figure 1.9: Plant and animal cell comparison

By having the graphic organiser on display as a constant reference point, the desired understanding for the lesson will be achieved.

What follows are some examples of other graphic organisers, covering the six patterns of thinking A–F, that you might recognise as useful. Hopefully you will recognise through these worked examples a range of possibilities for your own classroom and subject.

(Please note that they are for illustrative purposes and don't purport to cover every possible link or connection – the subject specialist would no doubt be able to add a number of additional elements to many of them.)

Pattern of thinking A: knowledge/recall

This type of graphic organiser is particularly useful when dealing with:

Description.

Lists.

Names.

Identification.

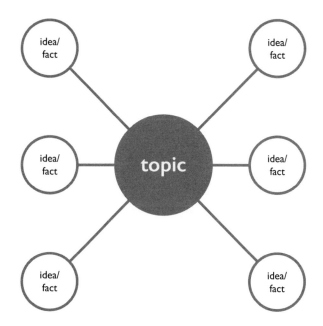

Figure 1.10: Pattern A

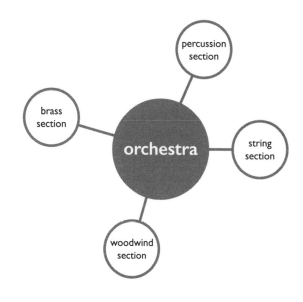

Figure 1.11: Pattern A – orchestra

In this example the teacher decides not to present the names of the instruments all at once, together with the names of the groups they sit within, as this would overwhelm working memory resources. The teacher has reminded themselves of some of the rules about working memory limitations. Here it is worth recalling the magical number seven (plus or minus two): present more instruments than this and it is unlikely that pupils will be able to recall them.

So the teacher would select this type of graphic organiser as the most effective one to visually communicate that pupils are required to recall the names of the individual items.

As there are far more than seven instruments in an orchestra (closer to 30 depending on the size of the ensemble), sharing the names of all of these instruments at once would clearly overwhelm working memory.

This type of graphic organiser immediately conveys that there are four major 'components' present within an orchestra. The working memory can process this easily.

The teacher could then introduce the rest of the instruments in chunks, a group at a time. For example, begin with the brass section and share the names of the brass instruments: trumpet, trombone, French horn and so on.

The following additional examples show how this graphic organiser could work in other subject areas.

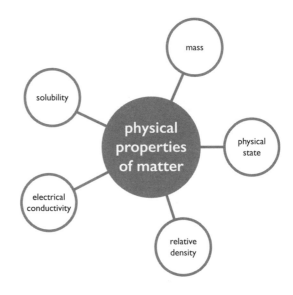

Figure 1.12: Science – the physical properties of matter

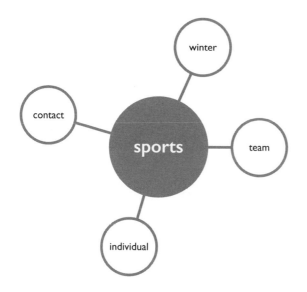

Figure 1.13: PE – types of sports

It's probably worth reiterating that these simple forms of graphic organiser are only appropriate for the novice. Naturally, over time, the teacher will want to expand on each of these elements. The teaching needs to become progressively more detailed and interconnected, just as the schema held within each pupil's mind needs to be expanded over time.

So, in our PE example, pupils will gradually learn the names of different types of team sports, contact sports, winter sports and individual sports. They will learn the rules and the skills required to play them. They will eventually be able to practise the skills within these sports, with the ultimate aim of mastering these skills (in essence achieving expert status).

This point is, of course, relevant for all six patterns of thinking shown in these examples.

Pattern of thinking B: sequencing

This type of graphic organiser is particularly useful when dealing with:

Ordering.

Method.

Processes.

Sequencing.

Steps.

Chronology.

Place order.

Timelines.

In Figure 1.15 on page 47, the teacher decides not to just offer a verbal exposition of how to work out the area of a rectangle as this would cause cognitive overload. There are likely too many steps for the pupils to hold in working memory.

Instead, the teacher identifies this diagram as the appropriate one to visually communicate the pattern of thinking required: the ability to correctly sequence the steps to calculate the area of a rectangle.

The teacher then takes a step-by-step approach to teaching the method of calculation.

Each step is taught in turn and the teacher does not progress onto the next one until the pupils achieve a high success rate on the current step.

The graphic organiser acts as a mental model for the pupils to follow of how to solve this calculation.

Again, the teacher is mindful to avoid overload by ensuring the number of steps stay under the magical number seven.

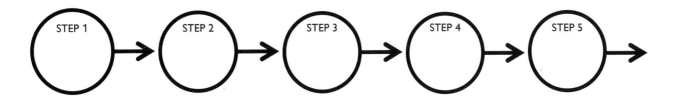

Figure 1.14: Pattern B

Figure 1.15: Maths – calculating the area of a rectangle using graph paper

Figure 1.16: History – timeline of key periods

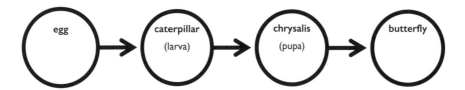

Figure 1.17: Biology – lifecycle of a butterfly

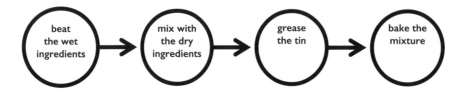

Figure 1.18: Food technology – stages of making a cake

Pattern of thinking C: cause and effect

This type of graphic organiser (see Figure 1.19, page 50) is particularly useful when dealing with:

Cause and effect.

Input and output.

Let's assume a geography teacher is delivering content about deforestation in the Amazon. The first option might be for the teacher to read a number of paragraphs of written text that describe several reasons why the Amazon rainforest has suffered from deforestation and then several paragraphs describing the effects.

Working memory limitations suggest that pupils will quickly forget much of what has been read to them if all they have done is listened to the teacher.

The teacher therefore selects this type of graphic organiser as it visually captures cause and effect. The direction of the arrows is crucial here too. They are

deliberately directed towards the central box to convey the idea of a cause, and outwards to suggest effects. Gestalt theory proposes that this is likely to convey the correct meaning and ensure appropriate interpretation of the diagram (see Figure 1.20, page 51).

This example attempts to test the limits of working memory by having three causes and three effects plus the issue under consideration in the middle making seven items in total. But it's the use of the diagram itself that helps to avoid the overload of working memory resources.

It would be far more difficult to detect these three causes and three effects within a sea of written text or spoken exposition.

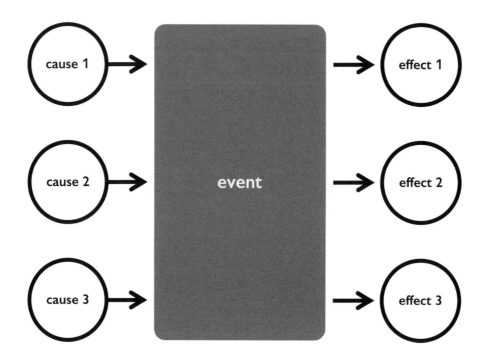

Figure 1.19: Pattern C

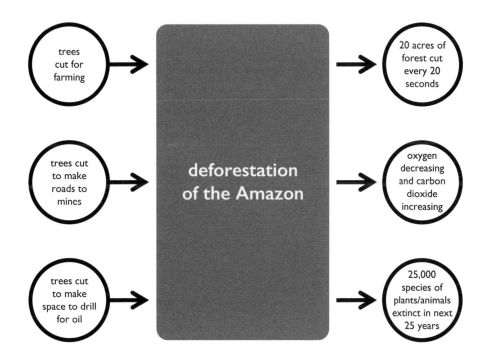

Figure 1.20: Geography – causes and effects of deforestation in the Amazon

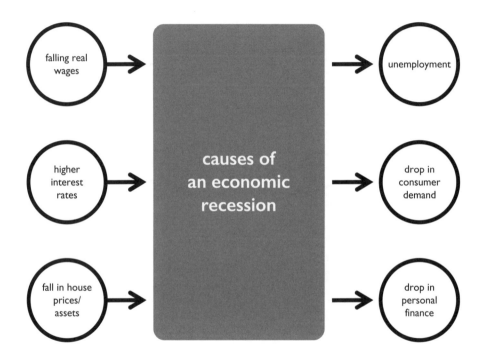

Figure 1.21: Economics – causes and effects of an economic recession

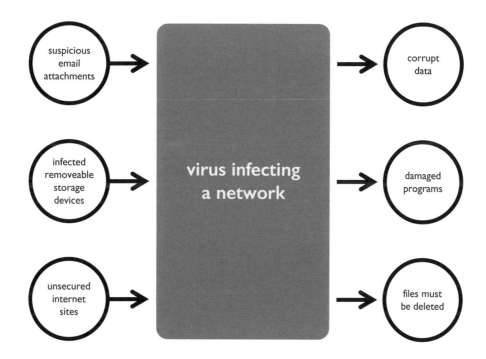

Figure 1.22: Information technology – causes and effects of a virus affecting a network

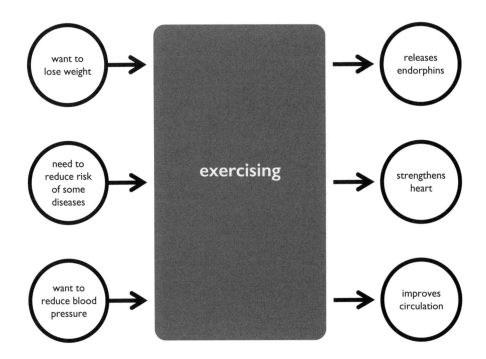

Figure 1.23: PE – motivation for and benefits of exercising

Pattern of thinking D: similarities and differences

This type of graphic organiser is particularly useful when dealing with:

Comparisons.

Contrasts.

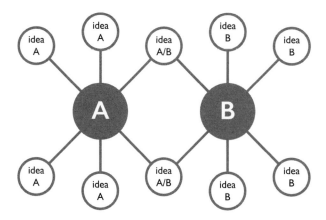

Figure 1.24: Pattern D

In a maths lesson, being asked to recognise the similarities and differences between two formulae simultaneously would overwhelm working memory.

It would be almost impossible for the novice to hold this detail if they received it through written text or a verbal exposition.

The particular graphic organiser on page 56 is very well adapted to some of the rules of Gestalt theory, most obviously similarity. The brain finds it almost effortless to 'see' them because of the deliberate and careful construction of this diagram.

So straightaway the pupils are able to form some level of understanding through interpretation of the connecting lines.

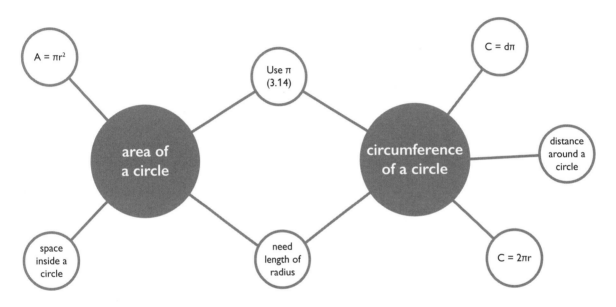

Figure 1.25: Maths — similarities and differences between the area and the circumference of a circle

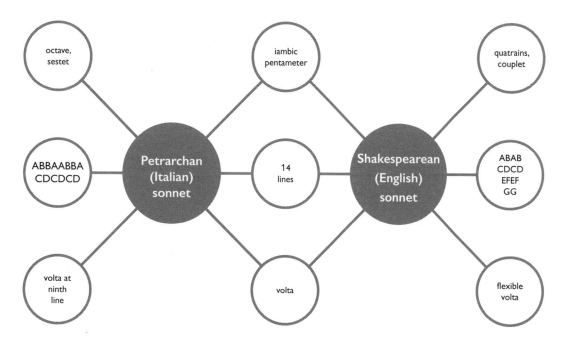

Figure 1.26: English – similarities and differences between two sonnets (Italian and English)

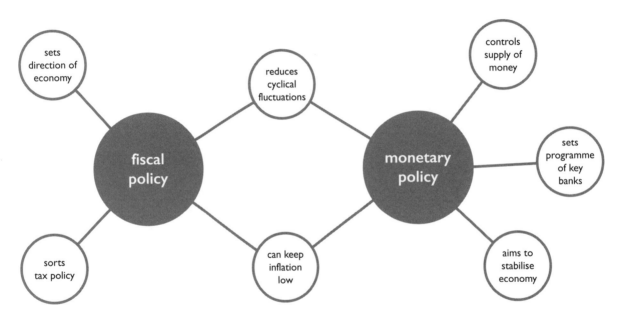

Figure 1.27: Economics – similarities and differences between fiscal policy and monetary policy

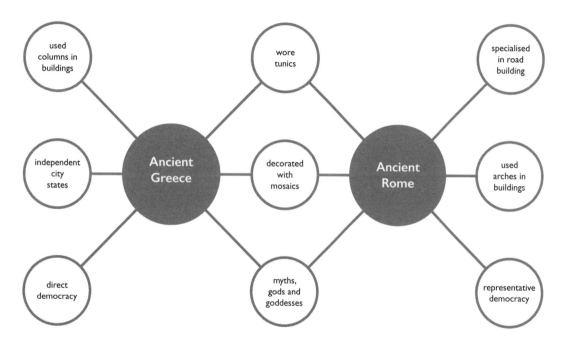

Figure 1.28: History – similarities and differences between Ancient Greece and Ancient Rome

Pattern of thinking E: classification

This type of graphic organiser is particularly useful when dealing with:

Themes.

Groupings.

Lists of similar items.

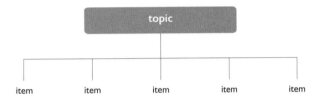

Figure 1.29: Pattern E

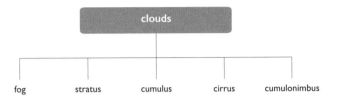

Figure 1.30: Science – different types of cloud

Straightaway it is possible for pupils to see that there are five types of cloud extending underneath the theme.

It is easy for them to see that all the component parts belong to the same major group. Generally, this type of graphic organiser is designed to separate knowledge groupings.

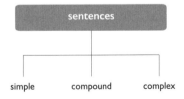

Figure 1.31: English – types of sentences

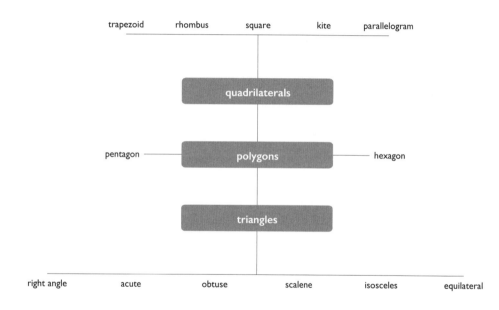

Figure 1.32: Maths – types of quadrilaterals

Pattern of thinking F: connection

This type of graphic organiser (see Figure 1.33, page 63) is particularly useful when dealing with:

Linking.

Interconnecting.

Joining.

As there are lots of interconnecting elements to the topic of marine biology the teacher has decided that this type of graphic organiser is the best one to choose (see Figure 1.34, page 64). The relationship between biotic and abiotic factors, and how they combine to produce marine environments, can be a very complex topic. This graphic organiser would make that relationship easier to comprehend.

Reflecting on earlier observations about the isolated elements effect, it would make sense for the teacher to approach this topic with a small steps or chunking mentality.

There is a strong argument for introducing these elements one by one, effectively hiding the rest of the circles and their content until it was appropriate to teach them. In other words, drip-feed the content.

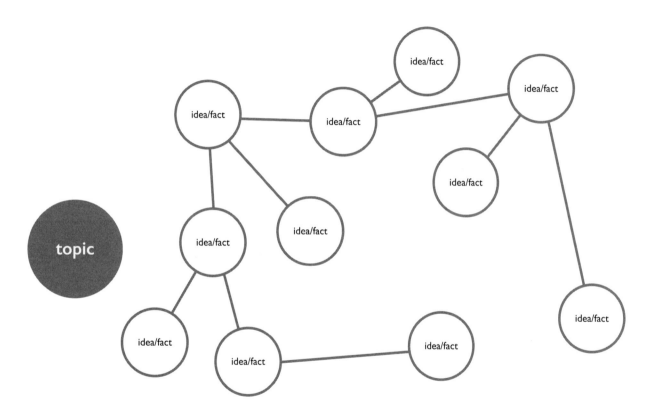

Figure 1.33: Pattern F

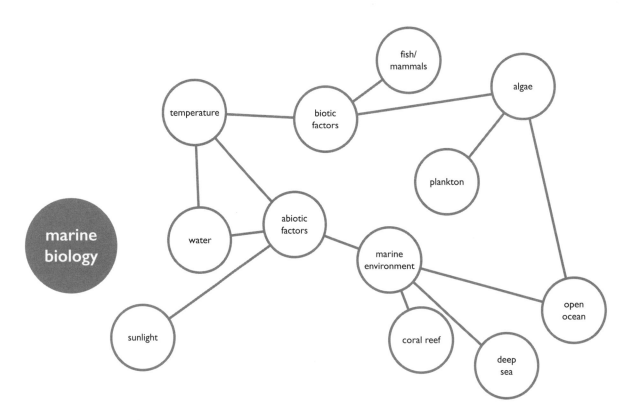

Figure 1.34: Science – marine biology

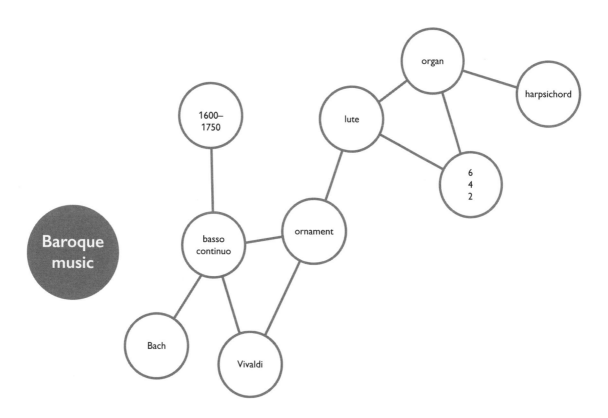

Figure 1.35: Music – Baroque music

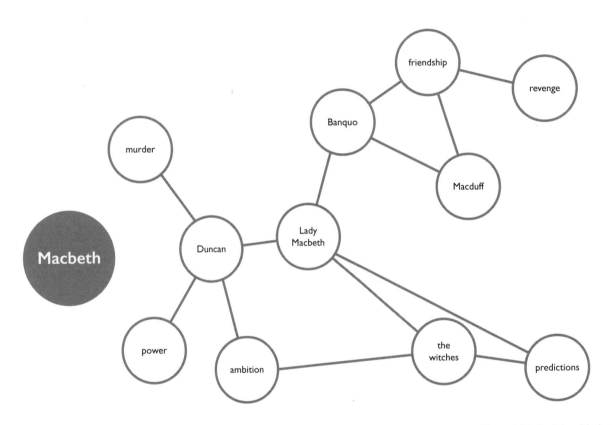

Figure 1.36: English – Macbeth

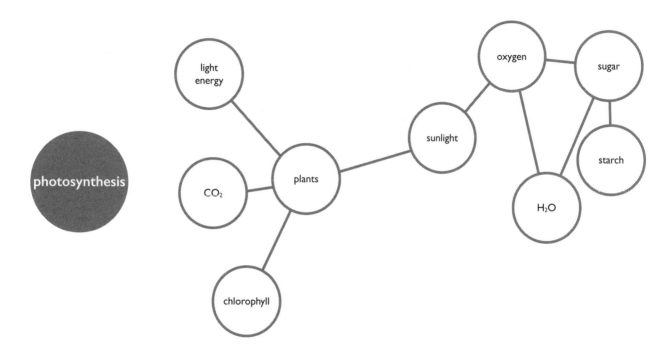

Figure 1.37: Biology – photosynthesis

Summary

Do

Consider use of a range of designs to suit the pattern of thinking required to help pupils construct meaning.

Design graphic organisers with a 'less can be more' mentality.

Ensure important hierarchies/themes are clearly communicated.

Include all relevant tier 3 vocabulary.

Adopt a chunking approach when teaching novice learners.

Don't

Overdetail or overcomplicate resources when teaching novice learners.

Teaching point 2

Teaching new knowledge/skills

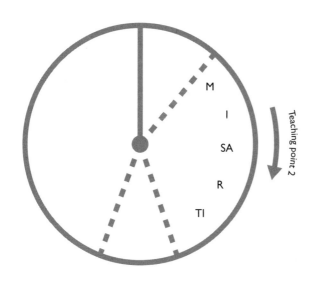

Figure 2.1: Teaching point 2

CLT effects to consider:

Modality effect (M).

Imagination effect (I).

Split-attention effect (SA).

Redundancy effect (R).

Transient information effect (TI).

Once new learning has been introduced (teaching point 1) then you can attend to teaching new knowledge or skills (teaching point 2).

Naturally this should expand and deepen the knowledge and understanding held within pupils' schemas.

Awareness of the modality effect and the imagination effect means that the teacher can potentially overcome working memory limitations and convey much more knowledge in lessons than would otherwise be possible.

Of course, this applies when the pupils are at the novice stage. Also, the suggestion is that the most effective means to convey new learning (when pupils are at this novice stage) is through explicit and direct teaching/instruction from the expert (i.e. the teacher).

Care must also be given to avoid the extraneous load that Sweller cautions against. This part of the lesson should, therefore, be cautious about the split-attention effect, the redundancy effect and the transient information effect.

Modality effect

This effect relates to the two systems operating within working memory, both with limited capacity. The technical terms are the 'phonological loop' – this manages the processing of auditory information – and the 'visuospatial sketchpad' – this manages the processing of visual and spatial information.

The modality effect is produced when one of these two systems is overloaded (i.e. it is presented with too many words or too many images). To avoid this situation, it is advisable to consider teaching approaches that combine both the visuospatial and the auditory systems *at the same time*. This can avoid overload in working memory.

The following example serves to illustrate how to avoid the modality effect.

Consider these words:

Upper bout

Neck

Strings

Bridge

Scroll

Tailpiece

Tuning pegs

For the novice learner these words are unintelligible on their own as a set. It is impossible to understand what they mean or to know the context to which they relate.

The novice learner would benefit from being given an appropriate visual together with these words in order to create meaning.

These words relate to the various parts of a violin.

To avoid the modality effect overloading working memory, the optimum method to teach the novice learner about the parts of the violin would be to show an unlabelled diagram and then orally share the new vocabulary with them, thereby creating a schema in the minds of the pupils. (If you are a novice when it comes to this topic, you can find the labelled version on page 79.)

Figure 2.2: Unlabelled violin

Some care needs to be given to the oral aspect of this lesson. It is entirely possible to think that you are utilising both the visuospatial and auditory channels to gain maximum learning impact, when in fact you might still be overloading working memory, allowing the transient information effect to occur.

To avoid too much spoken language, focus your oral exposition around the key information – in this example, the parts of the violin. We want to activate something called 'temporal contiguity', meaning that when we are exposed to two stimuli at the same time, we make a mental link between them. The term 'temporal contiguity principle' was coined by another eminent cognitive psychologist, Richard Mayer, and promotes the idea that learning is more effective if words and pictures are presented simultaneously.[1]

So make sure you speak the name as you are directing the pupils to that part of the violin. This way the pupils will make the correct association between the part they are looking at and the spoken name.

---

1   R. Mayer, Temporal Contiguity Principle. In *Multimedia Learning* (Cambridge: Cambridge University Press, 2009), pp. 153–170. DOI: 10.1017/CBO9780511811678.011

There are countless other examples of situations in which we should take account of the modality effect when instructing the novice learner. For example, when studying a Shakespeare play, watching a live-action or animated film version first makes it feel easier to digest and process the play, plot and characters when you come to read it.

The reason, of course, is that the images access the visuospatial sketchpad (the visual processing channel), and the accompanying dialogue accesses the phonological loop (auditory channel). The pupils do not have the additional load of reading text imposed on their working memory.

This is often seen as a strategy for lower ability pupils who might otherwise struggle with reading the play. What the modality effect demonstrates is that all learners would benefit from this approach if they have never encountered that particular play before.

This way working memory will not be overwhelmed as it will be able to connect new information from the written text to existing knowledge of the play gained *through* watching a film version first. Watching the film first will offer a broad framework of events and characters. But, just as in the violin example, care is needed.

The teacher should show the film in a series of manageable chunks, with a mini review after each one, reminding pupils of the characters and the plot as it progresses. Otherwise, by just watching the film in one sitting, the pupils would have too much to remember and so fall foul of the transient information effect once again.

Let the entire class of novice learners be introduced to the plot and characters in this way first and then introduce the text afterwards.

The teacher could easily 'trial' this technique as a piece of action research to see how it works. Ideally they would need to do this using two similar pieces of writing. The teacher would use their 'usual' approach to explore the first extract and then use the approach just described to explore the second piece. So, if we take *King Lear* as our example, the teacher might use another Shakespeare play or, indeed, a different extract from *King Lear* itself before testing the target

extract. It will work as long as you are comparing two broadly similar texts.

This is a perfect example of how schema acquisition can be deepened and strengthened. The schema, in this case, being the plot, themes and characters within the chosen play.

There are many instances of where the modality effect occurs in other subjects. Professor Sweller himself mentions an example of primary schoolchildren who had to read a temperature graph.[2] In the first experiment, two groups of children were presented with either audio *and* visual or visual only instructions about how to read a temperature graph. The findings were puzzling, in that the group who had only been presented with the visual instructions did better than the group who had been given both the audio and visual instructions. In other words, it appeared that the modality effect had been disproven.

2   W. Leahy and J. Sweller, Cognitive Load Theory, Modality of Presentation and the Transient Information Effect, *Applied Cognitive Psychology*, 25(6) (2011): 943–951.

However, the explanation for this apparent anomaly was that too much detail had been given in the oral explanation, along with the visual instructions, initiating the transient information effect.

When the experiment was repeated, the group who had both the visual and the (shortened and simplified) oral instructions did better than the group who had only the visual instructions. Therefore, as long as the oral input does not overload working memory, the modality effect will not overwhelm working memory.

Imagination effect

The imagination effect offers an opportunity to potentially circumvent pupils' working memory limitations and in effect 'cheat' them.

The essential difference between the modality effect and the imagination effect is that with the modality effect it is the teacher who provides the visuals to the learner (with, of course, the necessary oral instruction). With the imagination effect, the learner is required to 'imagine' the concept or process and generate the mental model, instead of it being given to them.

Sweller has shown this in an experiment with pupils aged 10 and 11 when learning about temperature and time graphs.[3]

The first group had to study the graph, whereas the second group had to engage in imagining the graph (essentially visualising what they could remember) after they had studied it. Subsequent test results showed imagining was beneficial to their learning – i.e. it supported better transfer to long-term memory than simply studying the graph alone.

Sweller also did this with groups of adults who were asked to study contour maps. The adults who studied the contour maps and then learnt through imagining did better on subsequent test questions. Again, it seems that the imagination effect triggers a

3   W. Leahy and J. Sweller, Cognitive Load and the Imagination Effect, *Applied Cognitive Psychology*, 18(7) (2004): 857–875.

visualisation dimension that assists transfer into long-term memory.

Thus, the modality effect and the imagination effect have been suggested as the principle CLT effects to consider when teaching new knowledge/skills to the novice in our hypothetical lesson structure.

We should, therefore, ensure that any new instruction is influenced by these two effects.

However, we also need to remember that any learning gains that might arise from utilising the modality effect and the imagination effect may be lost if we overlook the split-attention effect, the redundancy effect and the transient information effect.

Without care, it is entirely possible that we may inadvertently overload working memory resources by making choices that fall foul of these three effects when delivering new knowledge.

Split-attention effect

The first effect to consider, which may inadvertently create too much extraneous load, is the split-attention effect.

The visual dimension has been promoted heavily so far regarding its function in the modality effect and the imagination effect, but great care is needed in terms of *how* this information is presented.

Consider the two labelled diagrams of the heart that follow (both examples of a schema) on pages 76–77.

Without an understanding of CLT, there might not appear to be an issue with either of them. They both basically deliver the same information to the pupil: that is, they both label the main anatomical components of the heart.

Sweller and colleagues tested these types of diagrams and concluded that one of them places fewer demands on working memory resources than the other.

7. Superior vena cava (vein)
brings deoxygenated blood from head, neck, arm and chest regions to right atrium.

8. Inferior vena cava (vein)
brings deoxygenated blood from lower body regions to right atrium.

9. Right atrium
Receives deoxygenated blood via superior vena cava, inferior vena cava and coronary sinus.

10. Tricuspid valve
Prevents backflow of blood into right atrium.

11. Right ventricle
Contracts to pump blood to lungs via pulmonary trunk and left and right pulmonary arteries.

12. Pulmonary semilunar valve
Allows one-directional blood flow from ventricle to artery.

13. Pulmonary trunk
Divides into right and left pulmonary arteries. Takes blood to lungs.

1. Pulmonary veins
Carry blood to left atrium from lungs.

2. Left atrium
Receives oxygenated blood from pulmonary veins.

3. Bicuspid (mitral) valve
Prevents backflow of blood into left atrium.

4. Left ventricle
Contracts to pump blood to systemic circulation via ascending aorta.

5. Aortic semilunar valve
Allows one-directional blood flow from ventricle to artery.

6. Aorta (artery)
takes oxygenated blood away from the heart to the body.

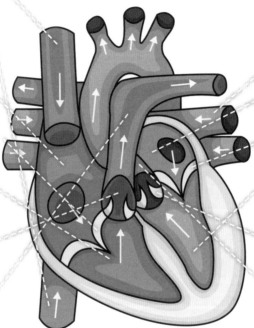

Figure 2.3: Blood flow through the heart – diagram A

1. Pulmonary veins
Carry blood to left atrium from lungs.

2. Left atrium
Receives oxygenated blood from pulmonary veins.

3. Bicuspid (mitral) valve
Prevents backflow of blood into left atrium.

4. Left ventricle
Contracts to pump blood to systemic
circulation via ascending aorta.

5. Aortic semilunar valve
Allows one-directional blood flow from ventricle to artery.

6. Aorta (artery)
takes oxygenated blood away from the heart to the body.

7. Superior vena cava (vein)
brings deoxygenated blood from head, neck,
arm and chest regions to right atrium.

8. Inferior vena cava (vein)
brings deoxygenated blood from lower
body regions to right atrium.

9. Right atrium
Receives deoxygenated blood via superior vena cava,
inferior vena cava and coronary sinus.

10. Tricuspid valve
Prevents backflow of blood into right atrium.

11. Right ventricle
Contracts to pump blood to lungs via pulmonary
trunk and left and right pulmonary arteries.

12. Pulmonary semilunar valve
Allows one-directional blood flow from ventricle to artery.

13. Pulmonary trunk
Divides into right and left pulmonary arteries. Takes blood to lungs.

7. Superior vena cava (vein)

8. Inferior vena cava (vein)

9. Right atrium

10. Tricuspid valve

11. Right ventricle

12. Pulmonary semilunar valve

13. Pulmonary trunk

1. Pulmonary veins

2. Left atrium

3. Bicuspid (mitral) valve

4. Left ventricle

5. Aortic semilunar valve

6. Aorta (artery)

Figure 2.4: Blood flow through the heart – diagram B

Can you guess which one places less demand?

The answer is diagram A.

The reason is that diagram B has effectively split the detailed explanation from the labelled diagram. The eye has to continually move backwards and forwards, find the appropriate details, memorise them and match them again with the label on the diagram in order to collate all the information about the part and its function.

Diagram A, however, has integrated all of the vital details in a single location (i.e. in each text box). There is no need to, firstly, identify the part of the heart and, secondly, seek the description elsewhere on the page (as in diagram B). All the information has been located under the part names in diagram A.

The key question we should ask when seeking to avoid the split-attention effect in our own teaching materials is this: have I integrated all the important detail in one place, or have I split it up across different points on the page?

If we want to be certain that we don't allow the split-attention effect to affect the lesson, we need to remind ourselves of the modality effect once again.

So let's go back to the example of the violin. The teacher wants to teach the class about the violin and, specifically, teach them the names of the different parts of the instrument. Awareness of the split-attention effect would suggest that diagram A is the correct version to use (if avoiding split attention was your objective).

However, as we know, the teacher has a third option in terms of how to teach the class this material which would be the optimum one to choose out of the three options available. This is because it is the one that places the least load on working memory.

The teacher could choose to omit all text labels from the diagram and just show the class Figure 2.7 on page 80.

The teacher would now orally name and point to the parts of the violin (i.e. utilise the modality effect).

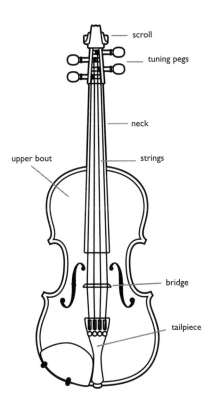

Figure 2.5: Violin – diagram A

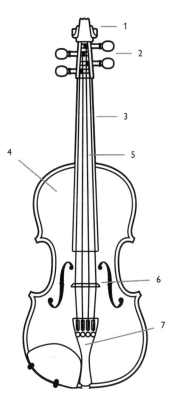

1. scroll
2. tuning pegs
3. neck
4. upper bout
5. strings
6. bridge
7. tailpiece

Figure 2.6: Violin – diagram B

This third option may feel counter-intuitive, as it might seem that without a written record of the new vocabulary the class will forget it. Indeed, of the three diagrams, diagram A may feel like the 'right' choice.

However, this is perhaps where CLT challenges our individual instinctual beliefs. If the split-attention effect occurs, then utilise the modality effect. This is described as 'double-barrelled learning' by Paul A. Kirschner and Mirjam Neelen.[4]

A meta-analysis has proven beyond doubt that teaching materials which combine images with oration allow pupils to learn more effectively than if the images are combined with written text (notwithstanding the caveat about avoiding too much oral exposition, which we have already discussed).[5]

Figure 2.7: Violin – diagram C

4   P. A. Kirschner and M. Neelen, Double-Barrelled Learning for Young and Old, *3-Star Learning Experiences* [blog] (30 May 2017). Available at: https://3starlearningexperiences.wordpress.com/2017/05/30/double-barrelled-learning-for-young-old/.

5   P. Ginns, Meta-Analysis of the Modality Effect, *Learning and Instruction*, 15(4) (2005): 313–331.

Redundancy effect

The second effect to consider at this point in the lesson is the redundancy effect. This effect can sometimes be hard to identify as it is easily confused with the split-attention effect.

Again, for anyone unfamiliar with CLT, it may not be apparent that there is an issue with presenting new content to pupils in the following way as in Figure 2.8.

The pupils are studying tropical rainforests. This slide may look like a well-intentioned resource that seeks to convey all the appropriate detail for the pupils, but it actually contains unnecessary additional detail that will overload working memory.

But why?

The answer lies in considering the information conveyed in both the labelled diagram and the lines of text below it.

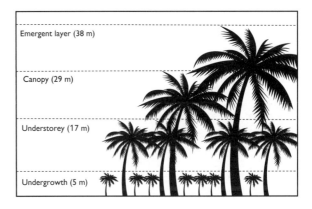

The diagram above shows the height of trees found in a tropical rainforest. The smallest trees grow to about 5 m high and are called the undergrowth. Above these are trees that grow to a height of 17 m, called the understorey. The third highest line of trees occupy the canopy, growing to 29 m high. Lastly, there are a few trees that grow above the canopy, called the emergent layer. These are the highest trees in the rainforest and grow to 38 m high.

Figure 2.8: Rainforest

Does the text offer any additional information not found in the diagram? The answer is no. Both show that the trees in the emergent layer grow to 38 m high. Both the text and the diagram describe the trees in the canopy as growing to a height of 29 m, and so on.

As a result, the teacher has provided additional but ultimately unhelpful information (unhelpful in the sense that it doesn't offer anything extra).

The text has simply replicated what the diagram is already showing. Therefore, this resource is guilty of the redundancy effect. The additional text is effectively a redundant element when the aim is to give pupils the information necessary to be able to describe the composition of a tropical rainforest. The redundant element requires working memory resources that are consequently unavailable for the task.

Other ways in which the teacher could inadvertently allow the redundancy effect to appear in this example is if they elected to read the text aloud whilst asking the pupils to read along at the same time, then the redundancy effect would apply. Too much working memory would be taken up in trying to listen to and follow the teacher as well as reading and processing the text for themselves.

It would be better if the teacher allowed the pupils to read it on their own first. The teacher could then read it aloud afterwards. The advantage of doing this would be that the teacher could be sure that the class have read and sounded out the words correctly and, if not, the pupils can self-correct when they hear the text read out by the teacher.

This a suitable adjustment when pupils have the necessary levels of reading comprehension.

However, if the teacher felt that the reading age of the pupils was too low for independent reading, then the teacher could read the text aloud as pupils are reading along. In this case, the purpose is not just to learn about trees, but also to improve reading skills. However, and crucially, the text would need to be read out in small manageable chunks as the pupils are reading simultaneously. This would not overwhelm working memory.

	Term	Scientific and geographical vocabulary
1	rainforest	A dense forest, normally found in tropical areas with high rainfall. They generate much of the world's oxygen.
2	country	A nation with its own government, e.g. UK, USA, Germany, Denmark, Brazil and China.
3	continent	The world's main land masses (Africa, Asia, Australasia, Europe, North America, South America, Antarctica).
4	ecosystem	A community of plants and animals that depend on each other to survive.
5	deforestation	The action of clearing a wide area of trees.
6	habitat	The natural home or environment of an animal, plant or organism.
7	interdependent	When two or more people or things rely on each other.

Causes of deforestation

1	To clear space for farming: growing crops (e.g. soya beans and palm oil) and space for cattle to generate cheap beef.
2	Chopping down trees for wood.
3	Clearing forest to drill for oil.
4	To build roads to access metal, gold and diamond mines.
5	To flood areas to generate electricity.

Impact of deforestation

1	An area the size of 20 football pitches is destroyed every 60 seconds.
2	Half of the tropical rainforests we once had are now gone.
3	28,000 species of animals are expected to become extinct in the next 25 years.
4	Local people's homes are destroyed.
5	Levels of carbon dioxide in the air are increasing and oxygen levels are decreasing.

		Location, layers and features
1	equator	Imaginary line through the middle of the earth. It receives the most sunlight.
2	Tropic of Cancer Tropic of Capricorn	Imaginary lines north and south of the equator. Most rainforest can be found between these two lines.
3	emergent layer	Giant trees that enjoy the most sun but high winds and cold.
4	canopy	Dense layer of trees overlapping each other. Home to most animals in the rainforest.
5	understory	Relatively dark, open area below the canopy.
6	undergrowth	Also known as the forest floor, mainly consisting of fallen trees, fruit, etc. that decomposes as food for trees.
7	flora and fauna	Flora = plants. Fauna = animals.
8	nocturnal	Describes an animal that comes out at night and sleeps during the day.
9	camouflage	Blending in to hide in the natural environment.
10	mimicry	Copying the look, sound or behaviour of something else.

1	Rainforests cover approximately 6% of the Earth's surface but contain more than half of the world's plants. About 90% of organisms are found in the canopy.
2	About 30 million species of plants and animals live in tropical rainforests.
3	There are two types of rainforests: temperate and tropical. Tropical rainforests are generally warmer than temperate ones.
4	Many things we have in our homes come from rainforests, such as chocolate, sugar, rubber, bamboo and many medicines.

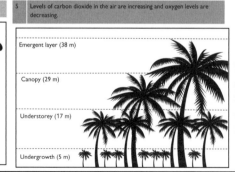

Tropical rainforests around the world

Emergent layer (38 m)
Canopy (29 m)
Understorey (17 m)
Undergrowth (5 m)

Figure 2.9: Rainforest – before

83

Tropical Rainforests

'the lungs of the earth'

KEY TERMS	CAUSES OF DEFORESTATION	IMPACT OF DEFORESTATION	LOCATION/ LAYERS/FEATURES	INTERESTING FACTS
rainforest	space for farming	20 acres every 20 seconds	Equatorial Tropic of Cancer	6% of earth's surface
ecosystem	trees for wood	50% of rainforest gone	Tropic of Capricorn	30 million plants/ animals
deforestation	building roads to mines	28,000 species lost in next 25 years	emergent layer	tropical/temperate
habitat	digging for oil	O_2 decreasing	canopy	chocolate, sugar, rubber, bamboo
interdependent	flooding areas for dams to make electricity	Increase in CO_2	undergrowth	
			flora/fauna	
			nocturnal	
			camouflage	

Figure 2.10: Rainforest – after

Redundancy occurs when there is unnecessary repetition. However, there is another way of thinking about the redundancy effect.

Broadly speaking, any detail that is not adding anything to the learning – that is an unnecessary 'extra' – can be classed as redundant information which ultimately adds to extraneous load.

Teachers should ideally become critical analysers of the learning resources that they share with pupils, and so hone their ability to detect examples of the redundancy effect.

We can learn a lot from the field of graphic design, and visual design generally, to help us here. Also, it is worth thinking back to the principles of Gestalt theory that we explored earlier. Equipped with this understanding, we can make changes to the design of the PowerPoint slides or worksheets that we create for our pupils.

Staying with geography and the topic of tropical rainforests, let's take a look at a before and after

version of a PowerPoint slide prepared by the teacher (see Figures 2.9 and 2.10, pages 83–84).

The question is, what should a CLT-friendly resource look like and what elements should it contain?

The before and after versions contain the same facts and ideas, but clearly the presentational format is different.

The critique of the before version is based on what a professional visual designer might say, informed by the ways in which the principles of Gestalt theory should be applied when designing visual information.

Critique of the before version:

> The use of text boxes, as they carry no meaning. Better to separate the sections spatially rather than demark using lines.

> The use of numbered statements is unhelpful and distracting as the order in which they are listed is not particularly important.

The use of various shaded text boxes is not helpful when the shading carries no particular meaning or relevance.

The lines are generally too thick.

The text is dense and compact; it's hard to read.

It attempts to squeeze as much detail as possible into as little space as possible.

The placement of text is random and chaotic.

Taking this critique into account, we might end up with the after version.

Reasons for approval of the after version:

It uses lots of white space.

The presentation is simple and clear: left alignment of the text and avoidance of unnecessary bullet points or numbered lists.

The sans serif font is without unnecessary flourishes.

Colour/shading is kept to a minimum (ideally only use one colour in addition to black and white, and only to support the identification of hierarchies).

Very thin lines are used to denote separation.

Icons are used to signpost key ideas/themes/headings.

Icons are kept small. (Ironically, smaller icons stand out more as there is plenty of white space around them.)

Some of the key Gestalt theory principles of simplicity, symmetry and proximity are certainly present in the after version.

When preparing a key resource and pursuing the goal of better pupil engagement, we can be guilty of (as I know I have been) using any or all of the following: an excessive amount of different fonts, numerous colours, thick lined text boxes and unnecessary visuals and cartoons.

If this is you, think again! Less can indeed be more.

So we've broadly focused on the use of visuals in the learning process, considering how to use the modality effect and imagination effect to our advantage, but we've also considered some cautionary comments linked to the split-attention effect and the redundancy effect.

For someone who is not aware of CLT, it is probably true to note that the split-attention effect and the redundancy effect represent a new perspective on how to present novel learning to pupils.

Questions that all teachers should consider include:

Is any of my teaching material guilty of redundancy or causing split attention?

Does any of my teaching material include too many additional details that essentially duplicate the knowledge already presented?

Does the design and presentation of my teaching materials follow the principles of Gestalt theory?

Transient information effect

The next effect that a teacher should be aware of in this part of the lesson (and, indeed, at any stage in the learning in which the pupil is a novice) relates to the transient information effect.

This effect relates to the point at which too much verbal exposition is generated by the teacher: much of that exposition is forgotten because it overloads working memory.

One of the dangers of this effect, though, is that it might seem to be so intuitively true as to not be worthy of consideration. We might believe that of course too much talking will mean some pupils will quickly forget the material.

Some teachers may claim that this is just common sense and has always been known.

Indeed, to paraphrase the Confucian scholar Xunzi:

I hear and I forget, I see and I remember, I do and I understand.

However, the transient information effect still needs to be recognised as something to keep in mind when delivering lessons.

Here is a scenario to illustrate why.

Consider walking past a classroom in which you observe a colleague working with their class. All the pupils appear totally attentive and are hanging on every word the teacher says. There are no additional materials available for the pupils to refer to, such as written text or complementary visuals to accompany the verbal exposition.

The teacher is relying totally on what they are saying.

Imagine that the behaviour of the pupils is exemplary too. Imagine that they are doing their upmost to absorb all the instruction coming from the teacher.

Some of the signs of purposeful learning appear to be present here: attentive, well-behaved pupils together with a highly knowledgeable and articulate teacher, 'teaching' them over an extended period of time.

However, in this example, CLT suggests the opposite to be true. The teacher is relying on the spoken word and nothing else. The spoken word is transient. There is no permanent record of what has been taught: the content, therefore, is quickly forgotten.

Care with the transient information effect is perhaps most needed with classes that are very well behaved and attentive as they may lull the teacher into a false sense of security.

However, what if the teacher has no option other than to verbally deliver new content because they have no access to any other resources?

Fortunately, there are some strategies that can be employed by the teacher. They could consider the following in order to avoid the transient information effect:

> If the pupils need to remember key points, such as a list or a number of separate items, then include no more than seven in this list. Ideally, five would be even better as the majority of pupils should be able to recall a list of five items accurately (considering that the magic number is seven, plus or minus two).

> If the pupils need to remember a series of instructions, give a maximum of three. More detail is involved in remembering instructions as there may be a number of subclauses within one instruction. Working memory limitations suggest that any more instructions and the pupils will forget what they are meant to be doing.

So imagine a teaching scenario, as an example, in which the pupils are being taught how to prepare a dish in a food technology lesson, thus forming a schema for the pupils. The teacher may have the class converged in one area to watch a cooking demonstration. The teaching proceeds via a demonstration. The pupils are watching and have no access to written instructions.

After the demonstration, the teacher then tasks the pupils with preparing their own dish. To avoid the transient information effect the teacher would:

> Only name up to five items of equipment that the pupils need for the recipe. If more than five pieces of equipment are required, then the teacher would chunk this list. For example, remind them of the equipment needed for the preparation of the ingredients, then later remind them of the equipment needed for cooking the dish, and so on.

> Similarly, no more than three oral instructions should be given at once. If more are necessary, they should be chunked in the same way as the first point.

The other way in which the transient information effect can impact on instruction is when the teacher, incorrectly, thinks that using the modality effect will allow them unlimited freedom to deliver extensive oral exposition alongside the visuals used in lessons.

In other words, they may assume that they are easing the load on working memory with the use of visuals *and* an accompanying oral exposition (i.e. utilising the modality effect) but they actually allow the oral aspect to extend for too long, so fall prey to the transient information effect.

This could *reverse* any learning gains won with the modality effect, because working memory has now been overloaded through extensive listening – and attempting to process which details are critical and which are additional – so there is not any space left in working memory to process any accompanying visuals.

The clear message to teachers regarding the transient information effect is this:

When teaching the novice learner, it is never a good idea to speak at length to them, especially when dealing with complicated information (whether you are using accompanying visuals or not). This is true at any point in the learning, not just when teaching new content.

The teacher instead needs the self-discipline to remember two simple rules:

1. The rule of three (for complex concepts or procedures).

2. The rule of five (for simple lists).

Summary

Do

Use visuals as a basis to teach new content to novice learners.

Follow the principles of Gestalt theory when designing teaching resources.

Remember the rule of three and the rule of five.

Don't

Allow teaching resources to be guilty of the split-attention effect or the redundancy effect.

Ask pupils to read long passages of text whilst you read aloud to them at the same time.

Talk for too long.

Teaching point 3

Checking for recall and understanding

CLT effect to consider:

Collective working memory effect (CWM).

The approach taken so far in this book has been to try to identify the point at which a teacher should be thinking about each of the 14 effects within a lesson.

In teaching point 1, we considered introducing a new topic. The teacher should be concerned with both the element interactivity effect and the isolated elements effect here.

Once this introduction is over, the teacher would then be thinking about teaching new knowledge to the novice learners. This is teaching point 2 and involves focusing on the following five effects: the modality effect, the imagination effect, the split-attention effect, the redundancy effect and the transient information effect.

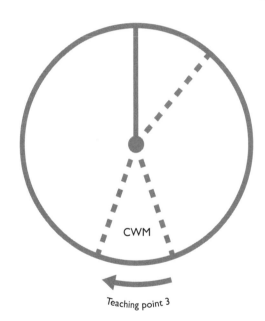

Figure 3.1: Teaching point 3

Now we have reached teaching point 3: the necessary input or teaching of novel information will be complete. Common sense might suggest the importance of pausing at this point in order to check for recall and understanding from the class.

Here lies the perfect opportunity for a short recap activity, and this can be accommodated by utilising the collective working memory effect.

Collective working memory effect

This is a relatively straightforward effect. It is based on the premise – in which we are by now well versed – that an individual's working memory is limited. However, when learning in a small group, there is an opportunity to share your ideas with others. As it is unlikely that all pupils will recall the same details, they will be able to learn more if they discuss what they can remember.

In other words, the collective working memory effect describes how more can be remembered when the pupils put their heads together: collective memory capacity will be greater than that which is held by an individual. An evaluation of the accuracy of their combined recall can be led by the teacher in terms of asking for a whole-class consensus as to the accuracy of what has been recalled, or the teacher may check by themselves by circling around the groups and correcting misconceptions if necessary.

As this effect broadly seeks to increase the load pupils are processing, rather than reducing it, it falls under the increasing intrinsic load category.

Before demonstrating how to incorporate the collective working memory effect into teaching, it is worth remembering the benefits of including a well-designed, short recap activity at this point in the lesson. The 'taught' element is concluded and the pupils are about to move on to a task designed to reveal their knowledge and understanding.

The first challenge for the teacher is to find out what is in their pupils' minds. There are, of course, any number of ways in which this can be done. Having done many informal straw polls with teachers, I know that many favour the use of the mini whiteboard for this task. Interestingly, Professor Dylan Wiliam described the mini whiteboard as 'the greatest development in education since the slate'.[1]

So the teacher could use their preferred method to elicit answers to quick-fire comprehension questions. Once the teacher has the information they need, they are faced with three choices:

1. **Move on.** If the information suggests that the class appear to have broadly remembered and understood what was taught to them in the first part of the lesson, the teacher can move on.

2. **Revisit.** If a number of pupils have revealed some gaps in either knowledge or understanding, the teacher would seek to address these.

Ways in which a teacher may seek to address any shortcomings might include:

Asking pupils to look again (they may have made mistakes through overeagerness).

Asking pupils to discuss with others what they might do to improve their work.

Prompting or nudging the pupils to help them understand better – offering a clue or a piece of advice.

3. **Reteach.** The recap may have revealed a significant gap in the knowledge and understanding of the majority of the class. Even though the teacher has taught it, the class have not necessarily learnt it! This might justify the decision to reteach the content and then check for understanding again before moving on with the lesson.

Looking for evidence of understanding allows the teacher to do what is at the heart of formative assessment: to know what the destination looks like and to find a mechanism to reveal the progress the pupil has made towards it.

---

1 Quoted in G. Gilbert, The Six Secrets of a Happy Classroom, *The Independent* (23 September 2012). Available at: https://www. independent.co.uk/news/education/schools/the-six-secrets-of-a-happy-classroom-2086855.html.

The magic is in the teacher who recognises that a pupil is further away than they should be and then, crucially, puts something in place to move them closer to the destination.

If the pupil is successful in moving forwards – as a result of acting on the teacher's guidance – then the teacher has narrowed the distance between where a pupil is versus where the teacher wants them to be.

Therefore, they have fulfilled the purpose of formative assessment.

With this objective in mind, it is at this point that the teacher could consider the collective working memory effect.

Technique: Listen-Think-Pair-Share with mini whiteboards

First credited to Frank Lyman at the University of Maryland in 1981, Listen-Think-Pair-Share is a collaborative teaching strategy that encourages pupils to form independent ideas, then discuss and share their ideas with others.[2]

This particular suggestion is a variation of this technique and combines the use of mini whiteboards with the Listen-Think-Pair-Share concept.

Step 1 (Listen)

After the teacher has delivered the new learning (which the pupils have listened to), they ask the pupils to sit in groups of four. Let's say our pupils are called Jenny, Paul, Matthew and Ahmed. In this scenario, the new content is about the London Olympics of 2012.

Step 2 (Think)

The teacher asks the pupils to each write down up to five things that they have been taught about the London Olympics. They can use text, drawings, diagrams or a combination to record their ideas on

---

2   F. Lyman, The Responsive Classroom Discussion: The Inclusion of All Students. In A. S. Anderson (ed.), *Mainstreaming Digest: A Collection of Faculty and Student Papers* (College Park, MD: University of Maryland, 1981), pp. 109–113.

their mini whiteboard. This is an individual task, so they should do this step on their own.

If the teacher anticipates that some pupils may choose to 'opt out' of this stage, there are a number of strategies to avoid this – for example, offering a variety of ways of recording their thoughts or ensuring that the initial teaching involves visual or auditory stimulus so they will at least be able to recall something that they have seen or heard.

Naturally, they may need to stress that this is group work and *all* pupils will need to make a contribution.

Step 3 (Pair)

The teacher asks the pupils to pair up within each group of four. At this point they will compare and contrast what they each have written.

In this example, Jenny and Paul are paired up, whilst Matthew is working with Ahmed.

Partner A begins by sharing what is on their list with their partner. Partner B only adds the idea to their own list if it's something new.

Partner B then shares their list with Partner A. Partner B may have remembered something which is not on Partner A's list. If so, it is added.

Ultimately both partners will end up with the same list.

Step 4 (Share)

Now the teacher instructs the two pairs to rejoin as their original group of four. Taking it in turns, they share what they have written on their mini whiteboards with the other pair. Each pair listens and notes down if they hear something from one of the group that they haven't written on their own mini whiteboard.

The key here is that by using all collective memories of the group of four, rather than that of the individual, more will be remembered. (Note the earlier comment about how to overcome potential inaccuracies within the groups.)

The reason the collective working memory effect is effective is because even though the pupils are in the same classroom, and exposed to the same input, they will each attend to and remember slightly different things. Inevitably, one pupil might remember something that another does not, simply because some things resonate more strongly with one person than they do with another.

This technique allows *all* pupils to benefit from shared memories.

The use of mini whiteboards means that these memories are recorded (not permanently, of course, but they are captured as a cue to use throughout the task). If the Listen-Think-Pair-Share activity was conducted as purely a spoken exercise, then problems connected with the transient information effect could occur.

The formative assessment dimension to this activity comes through what is revealed on the mini whiteboards. The teacher should be making judgements as they survey the class at work to see if there are any omissions of key details or misunderstandings.

The teacher could then fix any issues revealed through this Listen-Think-Pair-Share activity before moving on with the lesson.

This task also ensures the two key aspects of effective group work are present, which are:

1. Shared goals. (The group of four all made some contribution to recalling as much as they could about the London Olympics.)

2. Individual accountability. (By going from 'Think' to 'Pair' then to 'Share' there is no possibility that one person would 'carry' the rest of the group and allow 'passengers'.)

Summary

Do

Utilise the memories of more than one pupil.

Use this phase of the lesson as an opportunity for formative assessment.

Don't

Rely on pupils using just their own memories.

Ask whether there are any questions and move on if the class don't respond.

Teaching point 4

Pupils demonstrate understanding

CLT effects to consider:

  Worked example effect (WE).

  Completion problem effect (CP).

  Guidance-fading effect (GF).

  Variability effect (V).

  Expertise reversal effect (ER).

  Goal-free effect (GFr).

The teacher has now reached the part of the lesson in which they need the class to demonstrate understanding (teaching point 4).

This builds carefully on what has gone before. The constant reference to an appropriate schema reminds the class how today's lesson sits within a broader sequence of lessons (teaching point 1).

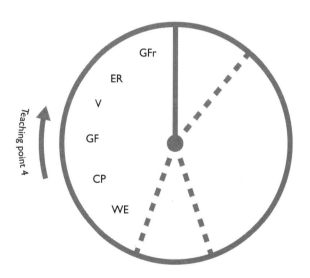

Figure 4.1: Teaching point 4

Additionally, the teacher has avoided extraneous load in their exposition and resources, so pupils' working memories should not be overwhelmed (teaching point 2).

Some careful checking for understanding occurred at the midpoint of the lesson via a Listen-Think-Pair-Share activity, so any major misunderstandings or omissions in knowledge will have been attended to (teaching point 3).

The teacher now must continue to think carefully to avoid overloading working memory in teaching point 4 – when pupils demonstrate knowledge and understanding.

Typically, the teacher would now set a 'big task'. Here we are beyond simple comprehension and recall; we want pupils to *use* their newly acquired knowledge. The task should require the pupils to think about a lot of different elements. Examples could include (and these are, of course, types of schema):

A skill.

A specific technique or set of techniques.

A method.

A process.

A mistake the teacher might make is to verbally describe a whole array of things that the pupils must remember to think about and include.

Pupils may embark on the big task, but, unintentionally, their working memory is already overloaded (in this case through the transient information effect).

Another mistake might be to ask the class whether there are any questions related to the upcoming task, and then proceed to let the pupils get on with it when no questions are forthcoming.

If the teacher considers the CLT effects presented here, they should ensure that none of the pitfalls just described will be fallen into.

If I want my pupils to understand what is required when using a certain skill, technique, method or process, it makes absolute sense to show them an example first.

One of the oldest effects studied by CLT researchers is the worked example effect, and it is a powerful tool for the teacher. In some ways it is an entirely intuitive technique. For example, as a young teacher in the early 1990s, I remember team teaching a class on the sports field.

The topic was rugby. I was explaining the different passing options that a scrum half has. The pupils appeared to be listening well enough but when it came to a game situation it was clear that whilst my instruction may have been listened to, it certainly was not understood!

My more experienced head of department was clearly watching this because he proceeded to approach me with the following sage advice:

> **'If you want them to know what a "spin pass" is in rugby, why don't you show them one first?'**

Looking back, this was my first exposure to the power of the worked example.

So, in this part of the lesson the teacher might benefit from reflecting on four particular effects: the worked example effect, the completion problem effect, the guidance-fading effect and the variability effect. We'll be exploring how one may naturally follow on from the other to see how they are all potentially linked.

To illustrate the benefits of these four effects, let's imagine that the teacher wants the class to learn the skill of writing to explain, with the aim of constructing a paragraph focused on explanation.

So the pupils are given the objective: 'We will be learning to write a developed explanation.' But the question they will certainly have is, how?

The ability to write a developed explanation is a high-value skill – one that's relevant to many subjects – and so it is a useful example to draw upon to illustrate these effects.

CLT suggests that the most effective approach would be to think about the worked example effect initially.

Therefore, the teacher starts by showing the class a worked example of a developed written explanation, such as this:

> **'In autumn, some birds migrate because hours of daylight shorten. The lack of daylight means that there is less food (such as plants and insects) available to birds, as those food sources need long hours of daylight to survive.'**

However, whilst the class have been shown a worked example, they will not necessarily know why it's a good example. Therefore, the teacher should proceed to break up this paragraph into four numbered parts and annotate it to describe what each part does.

It is done in the following way:

1. Statement of fact: 'In autumn, some birds migrate'.

2. Explanation connective: 'because'.

3. Reason: 'hours of daylight shorten'.

4. Development of reason: 'The lack of daylight means that there is less food (such as plants and insects) available to birds, as those food sources need long hours of daylight to survive.'

The pupils now, in theory, know the 'rules' of writing an explanation – i.e. that it contains four parts, which are:

1. A statement of fact.

2. An explanation connective, in this case 'because'.

3. The reason.

4. The development of the reason.

This works because they have not only seen a worked example, they have also been shown *why* the example works.

They are on the journey to becoming an expert in writing to explain.

Completion problem effect

The teacher can now build on the understanding the pupils have gained through the worked example effect. They would do this by showing a partial worked example: a paragraph with some elements missing, in order to introduce the completion problem effect.

In this second example, the teacher would only show some of the four parts required – for example:

> **'In spring, flowers bloom because hours of sunlight lengthen.'**

So, we can see that the pupils are given the first three parts:

1. Statement of fact: 'In spring, flowers bloom'.

2. Explanation connective: 'because'.

3. Reason: 'hours of daylight lengthen'.

As the teacher is now thinking in terms of the completion problem effect, they would ask the class what would be appropriate content to add as the development of the reason (i.e. part 4).

Collectively, they decide to add this:

> **'This increase in daylight means that more light energy is available for plants, which is crucial in order for them to grow.'**

The completion problem effect requires a gradual reduction in support. It will help the teacher to move the pupils from novices to experts, but not at the expense of overloading working memory.

Continuing with the lesson, the completion problem effect now can be merged with the guidance-fading effect. The teacher decides to offer a third example, but chooses to omit two of the four elements.

Now the pupils would see:

1. Statement of fact: 'In winter, plants die back'.

2. Explanation connective: 'because'.

However, parts 3 and 4 are missing, so the pupils would now have to complete the explanation on their own.

If they can do this, then the teacher could conclude that the pupils are ready to write a full four-part explanation independently. By this point pupils know that, to be successful, their explanation must incorporate the four parts with which they have been practising.

Guidance-fading effect

As can be seen, the completion problem effect is closely related to the guidance-fading effect, which is predicated on the idea of giving gradually reduced support to pupils as they become more expert. The guidance-fading effect describes how the teacher (after they have gone through several worked examples with the class) offers partially complete solutions or answers and encourages the pupils to fill in the blanks. Even something as simple as the use of sticky notes or correction fluid to hide some of the elements in an example can provide the opportunity for this.

To summarise, then, when it comes to teaching point 4, always start with the worked example effect as a solution to supporting the novice pupils in producing high-quality responses. This will avoid overloading working memory.

Then consider employing the completion problem effect and the guidance-fading effect as an additional teaching technique, as these effects will help pupils in their journeys towards becoming experts.

Variability effect

If the goal here is to move pupils from novice to expert, there is another effect to consider: the variability effect. This effect increases intrinsic cognitive load and so only works if pupils are already sufficiently well versed in the subject matter to be able to handle the increase.

In an effort to ensure that the pupils understand what is required from a developed written explanation, the teacher might elect to show several examples, rather than one annotated worked example. They would instruct the pupils to analyse them, find the common features that are consistent in all of them and, by doing this, unpick how to write a developed written explanation.

So the class might be offered these three examples:

1. 'In autumn, some birds migrate because hours of daylight shorten. The lack of daylight means that there is less food (such as plants and insects) available to birds, as those food sources need long hours of daylight to survive.'

2. 'In spring, flowers bloom because hours of sunlight lengthen. This increase in daylight means that more light energy is available for plants, which is crucial in order for them to grow.'

3. 'In winter, perennial plants die back because temperatures fall. This fall in temperature causes water in the plants' cells to turn to ice.'

The task is to find the components which are present in all three examples. This inductive approach means that, providing the initial work was done effectively, pupils will understand how these are successful examples of a developed written explanation.

As the pupils are novices, it makes sense for the teacher to maintain a consistent structure (i.e. four parts) but vary the knowledge required (i.e. spring, summer and winter).

The hope, of course, is that they will detect that each of the three examples has an opening statement of fact, a connective (in this case the word 'because'), a reason, and a development of the reason. The variability will show them the range of scenarios to which the common components apply.

As their expertise grows, it makes sense to vary the type of connectives to include phrases like 'as a result of' or 'due to'. This would convey that there are several connectives that can be used when explaining.

The focus on these examples revolve around the four seasons. Staying with the same topic area should assist pupils by making the connections easy to see. However, in this example of a science teacher (who teaches biology, chemistry and physics), they would

only really be sure that the class have understood how to write an explanation following this 'formula' if they are able to transfer this to other science lessons that focus on different topics.

For example, when teaching chemistry, the same teacher might ask: Why do metal alloys rust?

The type of response the teacher might hope for might look like this:

> **Metal alloys rust because of corrosion. This corrosion is a result of the presence of water and oxygen forming iron oxide on the metal's surface.**

It is only by transferring the skill into a new context that the teacher can be sure that the skill has been understood.

The table that follows seeks to visualise the transition from novice to expert. The worked example effect, the completion problem effect and the guidance-fading effect are all attempts to avoid overloading working memory for the novice. This is done by reducing the amount pupils have to process and think about (i.e. by showing a worked example they don't have to think of one that already exists from memory as well as construct a new one). This becomes a way of reducing extraneous cognitive load.

By this point the teacher might sense an increasing expertise amongst their pupils. Here it is possible for the teacher to increase the load on pupils by offering a range of worked examples of a particular problem or response. The variability effect, in contrast, is different. Here the teacher would give the pupils a variety of worked examples as opposed to just one. The teacher would select a variety of worked examples that all held some common features or aspects crucial to that particular type of example. For the pupil who has progressed their thinking and understanding from a complete novice (i.e. by exposure to worked examples), they could now have their thinking extended by finding consistent features or aspects within a number of worked examples, even if they appear different on the surface.

Novice to expert

Novice	Transitioning	Expert
The novice pupil is dependent on the teacher.	The pupil and the teacher are interdependent.	The expert pupil is independent of the teacher.
Teacher role: active – leads, demonstrates, shows.	Teacher role: fades guidance.	Teacher role: passive – observes, questions.
Pupil role: passive – observes, questions.	Pupil invited to co-construct response with teacher.	Pupil role: active – leads, demonstrates, shows.

Expertise reversal effect

If you have pupils who are clearly demonstrating the traits of the expert, then CLT suggests that there is a need for caution here. We now need to consider the expertise reversal effect.

Briefly, Sweller warns that whilst studying worked examples is an effective strategy for the novice, as expertise increases, worked examples may become redundant and will not actually add anything as pupils' expertise grows. Otherwise useful space in working memory would be taken up with superfluous worked examples when, instead, it should be devoted to problem-solving activities.

Let's stay with our example of pupils being taught to produce a developed written explanation.

The question now is about how the teacher can avoid the expertise reversal effect and instead promote a more problem-solving/enquiry-led type of learning.

There are some possible suggestions for a pupil who has become expert, in so much as they can routinely generate different examples of written explanations that follow the four-part formula modelled by the teacher in the earlier examples.

The teacher could ask them to generate their own examples of writing to explain, but to mix up the four parts. For example:

> **'The shortening hours of daylight in autumn cause a reduction in the food sources that birds need – such as plants and insects. As a result of this, birds migrate.'**

Alternatively, the teacher may ask the pupil to display more sophisticated grammatical techniques, such as the use of fronted adverbials. For example:

> **'Blooming in springtime, plants start to grow because of the increase in light energy.'**

In essence, the expertise reversal effect is best avoided by recognising when pupils reach the expert stage. When this happens, do not continue to give them yet more worked examples, but instead design a learning activity that seeks to extend their expertise.

The examples discussed here try to achieve this by:

1. Mixing up the elements within the four-part formula.

2. Introducing more sophisticated grammatical devices that can be used in an explanation (in this case, the use of a fronted adverbial).

Goal-free effect

We can now turn our attention to the last of the 14 effects which are under our consideration. Perhaps ironically, whilst it's the last one to be examined in this book, it was the first effect to be studied by Professor Sweller.

The goal-free effect seems to work most readily in subject domains in which number calculations are prevalent, such as maths and physics (in terms of evidence from randomised controlled trials).[1] However, once the principle behind the goal-free effect is understood, there is no harm in the teacher of literacy-heavy subjects trialling its use too. Firstly, though, we need to understand the effect.

The strategy works by removing the question from the problem which is to be solved. Instead, the pupils are left with just the information. The effect is best

1   F. Paas and F. Kirschner, Goal-Free Effect. In N.M. Seel (ed.), *Encyclopedia of the Sciences of Learning* (Boston, MA: Springer, 2012). DOI: 10.1007/978-1-4419-1428-6_299

shown when this information is in the form of a table, diagram or chart.

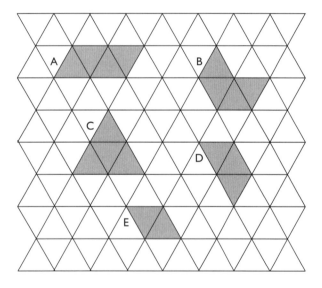

Figure 4.2: Goal-free polygons

So, in this example, the teacher would not set any specific questions to be answered about the shapes on the triangular paper but instead ask the pupils to note down as much mathematical information as they can that they think might be relevant.

Typically, the pupils will list things like the names of the polygons. Pupils may also locate lines of symmetry. They may even calculate the perimeters and areas as well.

Maths teachers who regularly use the goal-free effect comment on how much more pupils think about, and extrapolate from, diagrams and graphs than they would if they were just given a specific question. The goal-free effect is held up as a technique to promote flexible thinking too.

If they are asked to answer one question, the pupils will only focus on getting that answer right. Utilising the goal-free effect encourages much deeper learning.

The goal-free element of this task is getting pupils to explore the information without the direction of a question.

When pupils start with a question, they have, in effect, a specific goal and potentially much more to think about.

This is especially true if the question requires them to think about a number of component parts, such as an evaluative question 'Which is the most …' or 'How far would you agree …' These types of questions require a number of components to be considered and then assessed relative to each other.

They must also ignore anything that is not relevant to finding the answer. We can see how this might overload working memory.

The benefit of the goal-free effect is that pupils don't have to hold multiple pieces of information in working memory at once, which is what they may have to do if they were given a specific goal.

Let's look at how this might work in chemistry – although the suggestion translates well into any teaching context.

Coming into the lesson, the class have a task to complete straightaway, which is written on the board:

> **Goal-free starter: write down all the chemistry you know about CH_3Cl (chloromethane).**

Alternatively, for younger chemistry pupils the example could be:

> **Write down all the chemistry you know about sodium.**

Chemistry teachers comment that their normal routine would be to set a question that tests the pupils' knowledge and understanding of something – CH_3Cl or sodium in these two examples. They then become frustrated when a lot of pupils don't really engage and instead wait for the teacher to provide a model answer so they don't have to think for themselves!

Approaching the task in this way means that the pupils have to do the thinking but, more crucially, working memory is not overloaded.

We've looked at maths and science examples so far, but I did say that this effect could be utilised in other subjects. So, how would a history teacher – for example – utilise the goal-free effect?

Let's imagine that the pupils are studying the Norman Conquest of 1066. The teacher might ordinarily pose this question:

> **Who had the rightful claim to the throne of England in 1066?**

This question requires pupils to know about the three possible claimants and some details about how legitimate their claims were, and then to judge their relative merits.

In other words, the question gives them lots to think about.

CLT would suggest that this could overload working memory.

As we have seen, there is merit in approaching the task differently. Instead, the history teacher could write on the board:

> **List everything you know about the people who thought they should have the throne of England in 1066.**

The key, once again, is that pupils are not led by the direction of the question but instead are simply asked to reveal whatever is in their heads, one thought at a time.

Summary

Do

Use worked examples.

Consider *how* you are using worked examples: offer a variety, including partially completed ones.

Consider the value of not giving pupils too much to think about during tasks.

Don't

Over-rely on worked examples.

Conclusion

I'm sure that in the late 1980s Professor John Sweller would never have imagined that CLT would eventually be described as the 'single most important thing that teachers should know'.[1]

This book is an attempt to bring this theory to classroom teachers in an entirely accessible, practical and realistic way.

If you, or any teachers you know, remain unconvinced of the relevance of novice learners' limited working memory capacity, they could try the following activity in a staff training session.

Invite a volunteer up to the front. Ask them to only volunteer if they are confident that they can recall key personal details. Examples could be related to things like birthdays of relatives, the number of pets they have had and their names to the registration number of their first car or indeed any car they wish to recall.

Invite them to recount out loud each of these details in turn.

Observe as they confidently recite all of the details accurately.

Once they have finished, explain to the audience that the simple reason why the teacher was able to recite these details accurately is because they are well-known to them: it is personal information that the individual has had to think about lots of times. Multiple retrievals have simply allowed for automated recall, and as such the information is secure in the long-term memory.

As it's in the long-term memory, the teacher can draw this detail out and back into their working memory.

---

1   D. Wiliam, Twitter, 26 January 2017. Available at: https://twitter.com/dylanwiliam/status/824682504602943489.

This should demonstrate that working memory can cope with lots, provided that it is using information drawn from long-term memory. Indeed, no limits to this processing ability have been discovered.

Now let's change the activity.

This time, you are going to share your equivalent details with them.

In other words, the volunteer has to listen to you recounting your details. So, you would now recite the birthdays of your family members, the number of pets you have had and their names and the registration number of a car you have owned.

Once you have finished, simply ask the teacher to repeat what they can remember from what you have just said.

Typically, they will not be able to recall much.

The explanation behind the difference in recall ability is because they are, in effect, the expert on their own personal details. That knowledge is in their long-term memory.

However, when you shared your personal details with them, you put them in the position of the novice. Your personal details are new to them, so all the information had to be processed in their working memory. As working memory is limited in capacity and duration, they were only able to recall a fraction of the detail you shared with them: most of it would have been quickly forgotten.

The implication is that if teachers are unaware of the limits of working memory when learning something new, the quality of the learning that pupils experience will ultimately suffer.

The format of this book has been designed in such a way as to support teachers in thinking about when and how these 14 CLT effects should be considered in the course of a lesson or sequence of lessons.

As familiarity and confidence in understanding these effects grows then teachers will see that they can be applied at many different points and in many different contexts.

There seems to be a constant drive within schools to examine how learning can be optimised, and CLT makes a huge contribution to this effort.

Some of the strategies and research may appear counter-intuitive. If a pupil is a novice, why wouldn't the teacher want to supply them with as much detail as possible? This might be done with the best intentions, or, in other words, might aim to give the pupil the best chance of developing some level of expertise.

However, CLT suggests that the opposite is true. The limited capacity of working memory when learning novel information suggests that the mantra 'less is more' would serve teachers well.

The challenge then, of course, is to increase the complexity and depth of the material to be learnt over time: to stretch pupils that little bit more as their expertise grows. One of our ultimate goals as educators is, after all, to help our pupils become as expert as they can be.

This is the ultimate prize because from here choices are possible and desirable futures can be secured.

Finally, there is a lot of detailed and complex research literature available on CLT. Indeed, the original papers are available online. As teachers we should thank the research community for testing these effects and giving us the confidence that the data supports the conclusions and observations that this book illustrates.

This book has attempted to make sense of the research in terms of making it easily digestible for the time-poor classroom teacher.

If Albert Einstein did indeed say that 'Everything should be made as simple as possible, but not simpler' then I hope this book has followed that sentiment.[2] I hope it helps to disseminate the research behind CLT and work it into the practice of ordinary classroom teachers everywhere.

2   For a discussion of the sources, see: https://quoteinvestigator.com/2011/05/13/einstein-simple/.

References and further reading

Beck, I. L., McKeown, M. G. and Kucan, L. (2013). *Bringing Words to Life: Robust Vocabulary Instruction*, 2nd edn (New York: The Guilford Press).

Geary, D. C. (2005). *Origin of Mind: Evolution of Brain, Cognition, and General Intelligence* (Washington, DC: American Psychological Association).

Gilbert, G. (2012). The Six Secrets of a Happy Classroom, *The Independent* (23 September). Available at: https://www.independent.co.uk/news/education/schools/the-six-secrets-of-a-happy-classroom-2086855.html.

Ginns, P. (2005). Meta-Analysis of the Modality Effect, *Learning and Instruction*, 15(4): 313–331.

Kalyuga, S., Ayres, P. L., Chandler, P. A. and Sweller, J. (2003). The Expertise Reversal Effect, *Educational Psychologist*, 38(1): 23–31.

Kirschner, P. A. (2018). The Ideal Learning Environment: Evidence-Informed Strategies for EEE-Learning, presentation delivered at researchED National Conference (8 September). Available at: https://researched.org.uk/wp-content/uploads/delightful-downloads/2018/09/Paul-Kirschner-rED18-The-Ideal-Learning-Environment.pdf.

Kirschner, P. A. and Neelen, M. (2017). Double-Barrelled Learning for Young and Old, *3-Star Learning Experiences* [blog] (30 May). Available at: https://3starlearningexperiences.wordpress.com/2017/05/30/double-barrelled-learning-for-young-old/.

Leahy, W. and Sweller, J. (2004). Cognitive Load and the Imagination Effect, *Applied Cognitive Psychology*, 18(7): 857–875.

Leahy, W. and Sweller, J. (2011). Cognitive Load Theory, Modality of Presentation and the Transient Information Effect, *Applied Cognitive Psychology*, 25(6): 943–951.

Lyman, F. (1981). The Responsive Classroom Discussion: The Inclusion of All Students. In A. S. Anderson (ed.), *Mainstreaming Digest: A Collection of Faculty and Student Papers* (College Park, MD: University of Maryland), pp. 109–113.

Mayer, R. (2009). Temporal Contiguity Principle. In *Multimedia Learning* (Cambridge: Cambridge University Press), pp. 153–170. DOI: 10.1017/ CBO9780511811678.011

Miller, G. A. (1956). The Magical Number Seven, Plus or Minus Two: Some Limits on Our Capacity for Processing Information, *Psychological Review*, 63(2): 81–97.

Mousavi, S. Y., Low, R. and Sweller, J. (1995). Reducing Cognitive Load by Mixing Auditory and Visual Presentation Modes, *Journal of Educational Psychology*, 87: 319–334.

Paas, F. and Kirschner, F. (2012). Goal-Free Effect. In N. M. Seel (ed.), *Encyclopedia of the Sciences of Learning* (Boston, MA: Springer). DOI: 10.1007/978-1-4419-1428-6_299

Rosenshine, B. (2012). Principles of Instruction: Research-Based Strategies That Every Teacher Should Know, *American Educator* (Spring): 12–19, 39. Available at: https://www.aft.org/sites/default/files/periodicals/ Rosenshine.pdf.

Sweller, J. (1988). Cognitive Load During Problem Solving: Effects on Learning, *Cognitive Science: A Multidisciplinary Journal*, 12(2): 257–285.

Sweller, J. (1994). Cognitive Load Theory, Learning Difficulty and Instructional Design, *Learning and Instruction*, 4(4): 295–312.

Sweller, J. (2010). Element Interactivity and Intrinsic, Extraneous, and Germane Cognitive Load, *Educational Psychology Review*, 22(2), Cognitive Load Theory: New Conceptualizations, Specifications, and Integrated Research Perspectives: 123–138.

Sweller, J. (2017). Cognitive Load Theory, without an Understanding of Human Cognitive Architecture, Instruction is Blind, talk given at researchED Melbourne (3 July). Available at: https://www.youtube. com/watch?v=gOLPfi9Ls-w.

Sweller, J., van Merrienboer, J. J. G. and Paas, F. G. W. C. (1998). Cognitive Architecture and Instructional Design, *Educational Psychology Review*, 10(3): 251–296.

Sweller, J., van Merrienboer, J. J. G. and Pass, F. G. W. C. (2019). Cognitive Architecture and Instructional Design: 20 Years Later, *Educational Psychology Review*, 31(2): 261–292.

Willingham, D. T. (2009). *Why Don't Students Like School? A Cognitive Scientist Answers Questions About How the Mind Works and What It Means for the Classroom* (San Francisco, CA: Jossey-Bass).

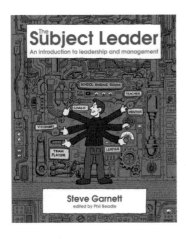

The Subject Leader

An introduction to leadership and management

Steve Garnett

ISBN: 978-184590796-9

The role of a subject leader is one of the most important in any school, second only to that of the head teacher. Subject leaders are working in the engine room of school life, expected to turn the vision, values and ethos of a school into reality.

However, most teachers went into education because they wanted to be teachers, not leaders, so they often haven't had any training into how to lead a subject area.

This book seeks to deliver a whole range of practical solutions to the challenges that the role presents. The areas covered range from setting and communicating your vision, delivering high-quality learning across all classes and developing rigorous and effective systems of self-evaluation to understanding and developing a transformational leadership style.

Hugely accessible and realistic, the book also tackles some of the other critical issues that sometimes face subject leaders. Practical solutions are offered around the issues of working with under-performing colleagues as well as managing the stresses of the role.

Improving Classroom Performance

Spoon feed no more, practical applications for effective teaching and learning

Stephen Chapman, Steve Garnett and Alan Jervis

ISBN: 978-184590694-8

Dragonfly Training was founded in 1999 and has established an excellent reputation internationally for providing inspiring, realistic and practical training courses for teachers. In this, their first book, three of its top trainers provide some of the very best hands-on approaches to teaching.

This book provides practical strategies that can be used by most teachers, in most subjects, most of the time – and offers insights and ideas to engage, inspire and motivate, including:

- How you present yourself in the classroom.

- Rules, routines and rituals for establishing effective learning patterns.

- Making your classroom the one every student wants to be in.

- Using ICT to the maximum.

Are you interested in getting Steve to come and talk to you and your staff about cognitive load theory?

Steve delivers exciting and inspirational training sessions for teachers on how to embed CLT into day-to-day lessons. His passion for and knowledge of CLT will help inspire your staff to take their first steps in this vital aspect of teaching and learning.

The best way to contact Steve is through Dragonfly Training Ltd. They have exclusive access to Steve and manage his UK and international training diary.

They can be contacted through their website www.dragonfly-training.co.uk or alternatively you may wish to email Steve directly via steveg@dragonfly-training.com